teen intervene

USING **BRIEF INTERVENTION** WITH **SUBSTANCE-ABUSING ADOLESCENTS**

SECOND EDITION

FACILITATOR GUIDE

Ken C. Winters, Ph.D.

HAZELDEN®

Hazelden
Center City, Minnesota 55012
hazelden.org

All rights reserved. First edition 2003.
Second edition 2011. Updated 2014 for *DSM-5*.
Printed in the United States of America

ISBN: 978-1-61649-195-6

Editor's note

The names, details, and circumstances may have been changed to protect the privacy of those mentioned in this publication.

This publication is not intended as a substitute for the advice of health care professionals.

The brain illustration in the document "Adolescent Brain Development" on the CD-ROM was originally published in Gogtay, N., J. N. Giedd, L. Lusk, K. M. Hayashi, D. Greenstein, A. C. Vaituzis, T. F. Nugent, D. H. Herman, L. S. Clasen, A. W. Toga, J. L. Rapoport, and P. M. Thompson. 2004. "Dynamic Mapping of Human Cortical Development during Childhood through Early Adulthood." *Proceedings of the National Academy of Sciences* 101: 8174–79. Copyright 2004 National Academy of Sciences, U.S.A. The illustration is reprinted with permission.

15 14   2 3 4 5 6

Cover design by David Spohn
Interior design and typesetting by Kinne Design

contents

Acknowledgments

The author wishes to acknowledge the contributions of numerous individuals in the development of *Teen-Intervene*, particularly Willa Leitten, Tamara Fahnhorst, and Andria Botzet.

How to Use the CD-ROM

Included with this manual is a CD-ROM that contains all the worksheets
and handouts you will need for the two client sessions and the parent/
guardian session. Also included are several informative articles written by
the author of *Teen-Intervene*. All the documents on the CD-ROM are in
PDF format and can be printed and copied for your personal use.

To open the documents on the CD-ROM, you will need Adobe Reader. If you
don't have Adobe Reader, this software can be downloaded for free at
www.adobe.com.

For a list of what is contained on the CD-ROM and for further instructions,
please see the *Read Me First* document on the CD-ROM.

AT A GLANCE: *Teen-Intervene*

What Is *Teen-Intervene*?

Teen-Intervene is a tested, time-efficient, evidence-based program for teenagers (twelve to nineteen years old) suspected of experiencing mild or moderate problems associated with alcohol or other drug use; the program can also include their parents or guardians. The *Teen-Intervene* program integrates the stages of change model, motivational interviewing, and cognitive-behavioral therapy.

Who Can Implement *Teen-Intervene*?

Teen-Intervene is designed for trained professionals, including teachers, school counselors, social workers, psychologists, and other youth-serving professionals.

How Long Does It Take to Administer *Teen-Intervene*?

Teen-Intervene can be administered in two or three sessions (the Parent/Guardian Session is optional). The program includes worksheets to help measure progress.

What Are the Parts of the *Teen-Intervene* Curriculum?

The facilitator guide, divided into five parts, provides a description of the uses of *Teen-Intervene,* an account of how this brief intervention curriculum was developed, step-by-step instructions for conducting each of the three sessions, and appendixes listing adolescent substance abuse screening tools, drug-specific information, frequently asked questions, resources, and references.

Forms and worksheets for the adolescent and parent/guardian sessions are provided on the CD-ROM and can be printed and copied for use with clients. All the materials to be used with parents have been translated into Spanish. These Spanish documents are also on the CD-ROM.

INTRODUCTION

Welcome to *Teen-Intervene: Using Brief Intervention with Substance-Abusing Adolescents.*

What Is *Teen-Intervene*?

Teen-Intervene is a tested, time-efficient, evidence-based program for teenagers (twelve to nineteen years old) suspected of experiencing mild or moderate problems associated with alcohol or other drug use and can include their parents or guardians. *Teen-Intervene* integrates the stages of change model, cognitive-behavioral therapy, and motivational interviewing into its program.

Teen-Intervene can be administered in two or three one-hour sessions. Seventy-five minutes would be a more desirable length for each of the first two sessions, which are individual sessions with the adolescent. Session 3 is an individual counseling session with the parent(s) or guardian(s) of the teenager. This last session should include a brief wrap-up conversation with both the parent(s) and the adolescent. A seven- to ten-day interval is recommended between sessions 1 and 2, and a ten-day interval between sessions 2 and 3.

What Are the Sections of the *Teen-Intervene* Curriculum?

Teen-Intervene is divided into two main sections: the facilitator guide and reproducible worksheets. The facilitator guide is divided into the following five parts:

- Part 1: Introduction (contains background information about the development of the program)
- Part 2: Adolescent Session 1

- Part 3: Adolescent Session 2

- Part 4: Parent/Guardian Session

- Part 5: Appendixes (listing of adolescent substance abuse screening tools, drug-specific information, frequently asked questions, resources, and references)

You will find all the worksheets and handouts needed for the adolescent and parent/guardian sessions on the CD-ROM. Print and copy these reproducible sheets for use with your clients. All the materials to be used with parents/guardians have been translated into Spanish. These Spanish documents are also on the CD-ROM.

Who Can Implement *Teen-Intervene*?

Teen-Intervene is designed for trained professionals, including teachers, school counselors, social workers, psychologists, and other youth-serving professionals who are working with drug-abusing teenagers. Users of the *Teen-Intervene* model should have formal training in basic counseling skills, as well as a basic understanding of the etiology, course, and treatment of adolescent alcohol and other drug addiction. Also, it is desirable that users have a certified degree in addiction counseling or a license in a related field of behavioral science.

Which Clients Can Benefit from *Teen-Intervene*?

The *Teen-Intervene* model has been developed for application with teenagers who display the early stages of drug use problems. It is intended for teenagers who are displaying or exhibiting mild or moderate problems associated with alcohol or other drug use. Such early-stage users often meet formal criteria for a mild or moderate substance use disorder; that is, they show harmful or hazardous consequences from their drug use. For example, the youth may be experiencing problems at school resulting from drug use or may be getting into arguments with his or her parents and friends as a result of drug use.

Teenagers who are not good candidates for *Teen-Intervene* include those who

- have a severe substance use disorder (for example, show loss of control of their drug use, have developed significant tolerance of drug use)
- are daily drug users
- suffer from an untreated psychiatric disorder, such as a major affective disorder or psychosis

In What Settings Should *Teen-Intervene* Be Used?

School Settings

Teen-Intervene is appropriate for inclusion in school-based chemical health programs that wish to add more services to supplement existing prevention and education programs. *Teen-Intervene* sessions are a suitable response for students with a mild or moderate drug abuse problem. In a study by D'Amico and Fromme (2000), a group of high school students were given school-based *Teen-Intervene* sessions, and the results were compared to those of a group who received the traditional DARE (Drug Abuse Resistance Education) curriculum. Students who had participated in the *Teen-Intervene* sessions had considerably larger reductions in the frequency of alcohol consumption and drug use versus those who participated in only the DARE program.

Juvenile Justice Settings

Alcohol and other drug abuse is a common factor among adolescent offenders, and yet treatment for these problems is not widely available. Thus, *Teen-Intervene*, with its focus on reducing resistance to change and increasing participant engagement, can be a valuable tool in this setting.

Mental Health Settings

Several adolescent studies indicate a strong co-association between psychiatric disorders and substance use disorders (Clark and Bukstein 1998). Brief interventions for substance use disorder, based on *Teen-Intervene*, during mental health treatment are valuable because such treatments are focused and can be easily integrated into a general mental health regimen for the client.

Waiting Lists

Adolescents who are on waiting lists for intensive treatment may be suitable candidates for *Teen-Intervene*. In this light, *Teen-Intervene* provides a therapeutic bridge for the client as he or she awaits more intensive treatment. The *Teen-Intervene* therapist can begin the process of increasing the client's readiness to change and awareness of the benefits of reducing or stopping drug use.

Why Use *Teen-Intervene* with Drug-Abusing Youth?

The development of effective, cost-efficient, and time-efficient interventions for drug-abusing adolescents is important, and yet it is an understudied priority in the health care delivery field. Pressures for shorter forms of drug abuse treatment are emerging from several sources (Winters 1999). Examples of these sources include

- historical developments in the field that encourage the use of such approaches within a comprehensive, community-based continuum of care for a broad range of substance use problems

- cost-containment policies in the managed-care sector

- the expansion of community-based detection systems, such as in-school health clinics

Research has indicated that brief interventions can be effective when treating adult alcoholics (see reviews by Bien, Miller, and Tonigan 1993; Hettema, Steele, and Miller 2005; U.S. Department of Health and Human Services 1999a) and with young substance abusers (Breslin et al. 2002; Erickson, Gerstle, and Feldstein 2005; Monti, Colby, and O'Leary 2001). Whereas brief interventions have many forms and vary in length (ranging from a onetime ten-minute session to several one-hour sessions), the approach described here is organized around a two- to three-session model that integrates developmentally adjusted components of motivational interviewing, cognitive-behavioral therapy, and the stages of change model. Key behavior change features of this model include the adolescent taking an active role in determining therapy goals, personalizing feedback to the client in the form of identifying costs and benefits of substance use, and establishing specific action steps that will facilitate the change process.

Continuum of Care Model

Adapted from Institute of Medicine, *Broadening the base of treatment for alcohol problems.*

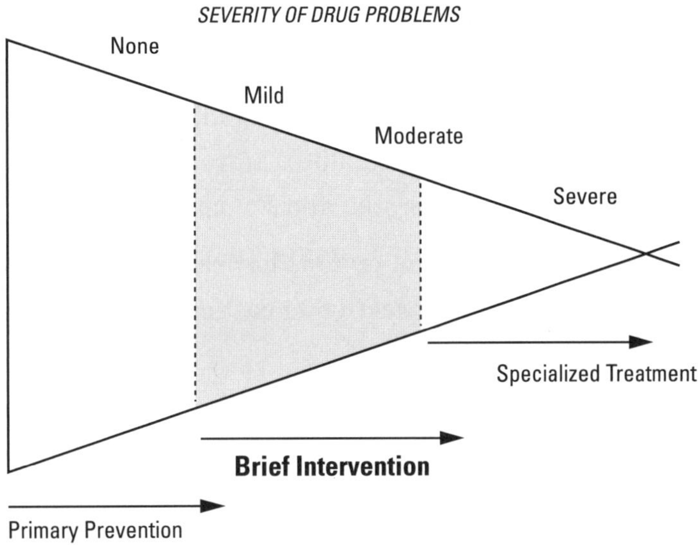

This figure represents a model for exploring how a continuum of care can be applied to treat a variety of drug use problems. The range of drug use problems is indicated on the top; responses to these problems are illustrated on the bottom. In general, specialized treatments, such as intensive outpatient and residential treatment, are appropriate referrals for youth with a severe substance use disorder. However, brief interventions, such as those employed in *Teen-Intervene,* are viewed as an appropriate response for mild to moderate substance use disorders.

Why Was *Teen-Intervene* Developed?

The impetus for developing this model is based on five premises.

- First, the gap between treatment need and treatment availability appears to be significantly increasing for adolescents, particularly for those with mild or moderate substance-use behaviors. Low-end severe cases are estimated to represent about 30 percent of adolescents who present for a drug abuse evaluation in Minnesota (Winters 2000).

- Second, this gap in service access is most likely the result of a tightening of treatment eligibility criteria by cost-conscious third-party payers.

- Third, with some exceptions, brief and relatively inexpensive interventions (for example, three to four sessions) have been shown to be effective as stand-alone therapies for *adult* substance abusers (see reviews by Bien, Miller, and Tonigan 1993; U.S. Department of Health and Human Services 2000). More recent work with youth is promising (Erickson, Gerstle, and Feldstein 2005).

- Fourth, lower-cost treatment options for less-severe adolescent drug abusers are potentially attractive to cost-conscious managed-care systems.

- Fifth, brief interventions make developmental sense given that (a) many drug-abusing youth are not "career" drug abusers and thus not very amenable to disease-oriented approaches, and (b) developmentally, young people are likely to be receptive to self-guided behavior change strategies, a cornerstone of brief interventions (Miller and Sanchez 1993).

What Are the Goals and Objectives of *Teen-Intervene*?

Abstinence is usually the long-term goal of drug treatment. However, to start in motion the process of abstinence, it stands to reason that harm reduction is a logical early-stage goal of *Teen-Intervene*. Any behavior change that reduces harm is a positive result. By taking on a more flexible approach toward goal attainment, defiant adolescent clients may be more receptive to the change process.

The *Teen-Intervene* model also emphasizes that behavior change goals need to be individualized. This feature recognizes the variety and range of adolescent drug involvement. Each young person has his or her own reasons for substance use, and individual teens may differ greatly in terms of willingness to change and treatment goals. By using individualized goals and personalized feedback, the treatment can be more directly focused for each adolescent's specific needs.

The *Teen-Intervene* model integrates a variety of techniques to establish behavior change goals with the adolescent. One strategy is to engage the adolescent in discussion of the pros and cons of drug use. This method helps the individual recognize that while drug use may have short-term personal benefits for the individual, drug use can also affect school performance and increase health risks.

The therapist using *Teen-Intervene* is instructed to be nonjudgmental, nonlabeling, and nonconfrontational. To put this in another way, the therapist's job is to act as a teacher or coach in order to help the adolescent progress through the stages of change. The intent is to move the client from low problem recognition and little willingness to change to the "action" stage, in which specific steps of positive behavior change are identified and implemented by the youth.

To summarize, *Teen-Intervene* is designed to help the client

- understand the treatment approach
- use the treatment session(s) effectively
- learn new skills that promote healthier behaviors
- take responsibility for self-change

Who Fills Out the Worksheets?

This *Teen-Intervene* curriculum includes eight different worksheets to use in the adolescent sessions. With the exception of the Client Questionnaire, all the worksheets should be filled out in collaboration between the facilitator or therapist and the adolescent. The therapist is encouraged to record the client's responses in the appropriate spaces on the worksheets. This will create rapport and a more cooperative environment, encourage adolescents who are reluctant to write, and enhance the client's motivation.

What Research-Based Theories Were Used to Develop *Teen-Intervene*?

The core components of *Teen-Intervene* are based on the following research theories, techniques, and therapies:

- stages of change model
- cognitive-behavioral therapy
- motivational interviewing

These components, also used in adult therapy, have been adjusted for adolescents. These adjustments include simplification of concepts, heavy emphasis on client engagement, and consideration of behavioral change goals likely to be relevant to an adolescent. Following is a summary of these components.

Stages of Change Model

The stages of change model, as described by Prochaska, DiClemente, and Norcross (1992), provides a framework to understand the motivational state of a client with respect to changing health behaviors. The primary five stages of change can be readily adapted to apply to a young person examining his or her drug-use behaviors. The chart on page 11 offers a description of how the stages of change model can be applied to a young person (U.S. Department of Health and Human Services 1999b).

Many adolescents in therapy are likely in the pre-contemplation or contemplation stage. The therapist or school counselor should recognize that this status need not be a barrier to change. Rather, the professional should focus on ways to help the young person progress to the next stage. One should not assume that a teenager in the pre-contemplation or contemplation stage is at a therapeutic dead end. Thus, the therapist should consider the client's ambivalence about change as normal and not necessarily stable.

Cognitive-Behavioral Therapy

Cognitive-behavioral therapy (CBT) is a therapeutic technique used to change one's perceptions, thoughts, and feelings about his or her behavior and to increase a person's awareness as to how social experiences affect the way we act. CBT is based on the principles of the social learning theory. CBT focuses on the importance of overcoming skill deficits and increasing the adolescent's existing coping skills by providing a means to obtaining social support.

The "ABC" principles of CBT are included in *Teen-Intervene* in order to facilitate the change process. The ABC model refers to an Antecedent that is responded to by various Behaviors or Beliefs and that is followed by Consequences.

STAGE	EXAMPLE	RESPONSE
Pre-contemplation. The teenager has no intention of changing his or her behavior anytime soon, regardless of possible negative consequences.	*An alcohol-using youth who limits his or her drinking to social situations and has experienced only minimal alcohol-related consequences.*	Provide information about the connection between possible problems and consequences of continued alcohol use. Include information about the harmful effects of alcohol on judgment, driving skills, etc.
Contemplation. The youth has begun to recognize some negative consequences related to his or her drug abuse. Change has not been affirmed or committed to.	*A teenager who has several negative consequences as a result of his or her use. The individual understands some of the dangers of using but has not made a decision to cut down or stop using.*	Examine indecisiveness by helping the young person recognize the costs of his or her drug use.
Preparation. The adolescent has decided to change his or her drug-using behavior and has made preparations for this change.	*The teenager has decided to reduce or stop using and makes a commitment to get help with this choice.*	Improvement of the intentions toward change is needed. A brief intervention can be useful in providing options for change.
Action. The adolescent puts forth the effort to continue a plan for change. Some signs of progress are observed in terms of attitude and behavior.	*The youth receives counseling or therapy. Thoughts of continued use may still be present, so relapse prevention is important.*	Develop and maintain a plan of action. Brief interventions can be used to support positive change, prevent relapse, and connect the adolescent with recovery-supporting resources.
Maintenance. New, healthier behaviors are in place. Long-term objectives are being considered and planned.	*A teenager who is receiving counseling or self-help on a regular basis, has found a sponsor, has made new sober friends, and has found replacement activities that revolve around sobriety.*	Prevention of a relapse is the main objective. A brief intervention can be used to help provide encouragement to maintain sobriety.

For example, a student may receive a low score on a test (Antecedent). This student may believe that he or she cannot be successful in school (Belief) and then act out (Behavior) in frustration. As a result, the student may incur punishment by school officials (Consequences). By applying specific therapeutic steps outlined in this facilitator guide, such as assessing high-risk situations and identifying errors in thinking that may contribute to bad decisions, the therapist or counselor helps the young person choose attitudes and behaviors that are alternatives to drug use.

Motivational Interviewing

Motivational interviewing or motivational enhancement is a therapy technique designed to enhance the adolescent's motivation to change some specified behavior. This curriculum for the *Teen-Intervene* model has incorporated many features of motivational interviewing.

Miller and Rollnick (2002) have identified key elements that are important to the successful application of motivational interviewing. An intervention that contains even some of these elements has been proven effective in instigating change and reducing drug use (Bien, Miller, and Tonigan 1993). These elements are

- personalizing feedback about the adolescent's problems and willingness to change

- emphasizing the point that change is the adolescent's responsibility

- providing specific and action-oriented recommendations on how to change, including a list of alternative behaviors

- conducting oneself as an empathetic therapist

- encouraging self-efficacy or optimism in the adolescent

Descriptions of each of these central elements of effective motivational interviewing follow.

- PERSONALIZED FEEDBACK
  Personalized feedback should be offered in a way that shows respect as well as cultural and individual sensitivity. The therapist who maintains a nonconfrontational and nonlabeling approach will facilitate

this process. Feedback is not to be used to "prove" that the adolescent has a drug use problem; rather, it is to help the young person recognize that change is in order. In the *Teen-Intervene* model, the client along with the therapist completes various assessments and worksheets to encourage the feedback process.

- PARTICIPANT'S RESPONSIBILITY
  The model emphasizes that the adolescent is ultimately responsible for choosing what to do about his or her drug-use behaviors. Thus, the therapist's goals are not forced upon the client. In this light, the therapist offers information, provides guidance and suggestions, and seeks a commitment from the client about what changes he or she will make.

  For example, in adolescent session 1, one of the initial statements from the therapist to the client is this: "I am not going to tell you what to do; only you can decide what you will do. But I would like to find out what you think about using alcohol or other drugs and maybe see if together we can come up with some ways to avoid problems in the future. You are the only one who will decide what happens with your use of alcohol or other drugs. If you choose, you can continue using the way that you have been. Or you can make a change. The choice is yours."

  When the adolescent is permitted to make his or her own choices about change, several positive expectations for change are set in motion, including that the client sees that change is primarily his or her responsibility, and if change occurs, self-efficacy is enhanced.

- RECOMMENDATIONS AND ALTERNATIVES FOR CHANGE
  Recommendations for change within the *Teen-Intervene* model are offered as advice to the client, not as rigid prescriptions of change that reflect the therapist's philosophy. Of course, the therapist can ask the client if he or she is interested in hearing the therapist's suggestions, but such information should be communicated in a nondogmatic manner.

  A list of alternative behaviors to drug use is provided in this facilitator guide. The idea is to offer the adolescent a variety of choices that can replace former patterns of behavior in specific situations. For example, an exercise is described to help the client think of specific alternatives to "just saying no" to alcohol or other drugs.

The pros and cons exercise is a primary technique described in the model to assist with the process of establishing specific goals. This exercise involves encouraging the client to examine the pros and cons of his or her substance use. It is from the con list that the therapist, with the client, can develop specific action goals for change.

- THERAPIST EMPATHY
  Reflective listening skills are an important part of motivational interviewing. The therapist is encouraged to create a safe environment that allows the young person to feel comfortable talking about personal matters. Statements such as "I understand what you are saying and I am not going to judge you on this" or "What do you see as the next step for yourself?" are effective empathetic statements. Other examples are included in each of the adolescent sessions.

- SELF-EFFICACY SKILLS
  Self-efficacy refers to the feeling of accomplishment within the adolescent. The change process is enhanced when clients feel that self-improvement is based on their accomplishments. The *Teen-Intervene* model incorporates several features that encourage client self-efficacy, such as having the therapist acknowledge positive change—no matter how small—and reminding the client that the therapy goals are the client's responsibility.

What Concerns Should I Be Aware Of?

As in any counseling setting with a young person, it is important that the adolescent client be fully advised that if he or she discloses being a victim of physical or sexual abuse, or reports that he or she may harm himself or herself, or another, the therapist is required to report such information to the proper authorities.

The therapist is also advised to obtain written consent from the parent prior to implementing *Teen-Intervene* when working with teenagers younger than eighteen years old. The consent form should describe the

Teen-Intervene procedures and the goals of the counseling sessions, and it should state that the therapist is mandated to report to proper authorities any disclosure by the youth of physical or sexual abuse. A sample Parent/Guardian Consent Form is included on the CD-ROM for your use.

This final caution is a reminder of the limitations of the *Teen-Intervene* approaches. The model described in this manual is not appropriate as a stand-alone therapy for teenagers with a severe substance use disorder. Such youth are likely to require a more intensive treatment program. Also, when abstinence is the only goal of treatment, *Teen-Intervene* may not be an appropriate treatment choice. This is not to say that *Teen-Intervene* treatment cannot strive for an abstinence goal. Abstinence is an ultimate goal for nearly all drug-abusing teenagers. But *Teen-Intervene* is designed so that it is appropriate for short-term goals that include risk elimination, risk reduction, and pattern normalization, in the context that abstinence is a long-term goal.

ADOLESCENT SESSION 1

INTRODUCTION

Welcome to adolescent session 1.

The purpose of session 1 is to help the client evaluate his or her alcohol and/or other drug use and to help him or her take steps toward the decision to quit using.

Goals of This Session:

During this session, the client will

- be introduced to the *Teen-Intervene* program

- complete an overview of his or her drug use history, as well as a measure of his or her readiness for change

- discuss the pros and cons of his or her chemical use

- evaluate how willing he or she is to change

- set goals around reducing or eliminating his or her chemical use

Time Required: 60–75 minutes

Materials Needed:

The following worksheets and handouts are located on the CD-ROM:

- Parent/Guardian Consent Form

- Client Questionnaire, including a scoring sheet for part 2 (PRQ)

- Pros and Cons Worksheet

- Triggers and Cravings Worksheet

- Ready to Change Worksheet 1

- Establish Goals Worksheet
- What Sets Off Your Alcohol and/or Other Drug Use? Worksheet
- Advantages of Not Using Drugs

Preparation Needed:

1. Read through all of session 1 so you are comfortable presenting it to the client.

2. Print and photocopy all worksheets (one copy for use with each client).

3. Have parent(s)/guardian(s) fill out and return the consent form.

4. Familiarize yourself with the administration and scoring of assessment tools (Client Questionnaire).

Background Information:

Establishing rapport with the participant at the outset of therapy is vital to the change process. Rapport building can be accomplished by

- using reflective listening skills
- being nonjudgmental
- asking questions to help investigate the positive and negative consequences of the substance-abusing behavior

The following is an outline for conducting session 1 in nine steps. Instructions, helpful hints, and suggested time frames for each step are included, along with a suggested script.

Note: Among the worksheets, the client should fill out only the Client Questionnaire. The therapist should fill out all other worksheets as he or she records the client's answers during the session.

SESSION OUTLINE

STEP 1:

Discuss the basic elements of the *Teen-Intervene* program with the client (10 MINUTES)

1. Welcome the client to the first session. Introduce yourself if the client does not know you.

2. Start the opening session by clarifying the basic elements of *Teen-Intervene*. Briefly discuss the following components identified by Monti and colleagues (2001):

   - the overall purpose and content of the intervention

   - the counselor's role, with an emphasis on what the counselor will and will not do in the sessions

   - issues of confidentiality; that is, if the client shows a risk for harming himself or herself or others, or is being abused by others (physically or sexually), it must be reported by the therapist

   - a description of program-specific elements, such as requirements of attendance and number of sessions

3. Use any of the following statements to illustrate how you can cover these introductory elements in a nonjudgmental approach:

   "What I would like to do is explore your use of alcohol and other drugs with you. We are concerned about teenage drug use and about the kinds of things that happen when young people have been using."

   "I am not going to tell you what to do; only you can decide what you will do. But I would like to find out what you think about using drugs and/or alcohol and maybe see if together we can come up with some ways to avoid problems in the future. You are the only one who will decide what happens with your use of drugs and/or alcohol. If you choose, you can continue using the way that you have been. Or you can make a change. The choice is yours."

   "Is this okay? Can we try this out?"

STEP 2:

Administer the Client Questionnaire (10 MINUTES)

1. Create rapport with the adolescent by presenting a simple overview and purpose of the questionnaire. The following is an example of what the therapist or counselor might say to introduce the questionnaire.

    "To help us get a better idea of how we want to proceed, I would like you to take this short questionnaire. It will only take five minutes. We will review the results together later in this session."

2. Collect and review pertinent background information about the client's drug and/or alcohol use. It is recommended that the counselor use the enclosed screening tool (Client Questionnaire), which provides an overview of the client's drug use history as well as a measure of the client's readiness for change.

3. Have the adolescent complete parts 1 and 2 of the Client Questionnaire. For the facilitator's convenience, a sample of this worksheet follows on page 21.

    This is the only client form that is self-administered and filled out by the client. For all other worksheets used with the client, the therapist will record the client's responses to the questions. It is recommended that the client complete the questionnaire during the session, not outside the office while waiting for his or her appointment. This will help create context and connection between the therapist and client.

4. Using the instructions on page 22, score part 2 of the Client Questionnaire—PRQ (problem recognition questionnaire)—promptly by hand, using a calculator if you wish. Once you are accustomed to calculating the results of the questionnaire, you will need only a minute or two. The PRQ produces a measure of the client's degree of willingness to change (low, medium, or high).

Sample of Client Questionnaire

Page 1 of 4

teen intervene

••• CLIENT QUESTIONNAIRE •••

NAME / ID: _______________________________   DATE: _______________

- ✔ This questionnaire asks about you and your experiences. Some questions ask how often you have used alcohol and other drugs. Others ask how much you agree with a statement.
- ✔ Please read each question carefully. Circle the answer that is right for you.
- ✔ Please answer every question.

Part 1 of Client Questionnaire

During the past twelve months, how many times (if any)

	Never	1–2	3–5	6–9	10–19	20–39	40+
1. Have you had alcoholic beverages (including beer, wine, and liquor) to drink?	1	2	3	4	5	6	7
2. Have you used marijuana (grass, weed, pot) or hashish (hash, hash oil)?	1	2	3	4	5	6	7
3. Have you used drugs other than alcohol and marijuana? *(Do not include if a doctor told you to take the drug.)*	1	2	3	4	5	6	7

continued on next page

1 of 4

Page 2 of 4

••• CLIENT QUESTIONNAIRE •••

If you have used other drugs, put an X in the space next to each drug that you have used at least **once during the past twelve months.** Do *not* include if a doctor told you to take it.

- _____ cocaine (coke, crack)
- _____ amphetamines (such as uppers, speed, meth, crank, bennies)
- _____ barbiturates (such as downs, goofballs, yellows, blues)
- _____ heroin (smack, horse, skag)
- _____ other narcotics (such as methadone, opium, morphine, codeine, Demerol, OxyContin, Percocet)
- _____ tranquilizers or sedatives (such as Librium, Valium, Xanax, Tuina)
- _____ psychedelics (such as LSD, PCP, mescaline, peyote)
- _____ inhalants (such as glue, aerosol cans, gases, correction fluid)
- _____ club drugs (Ecstasy, MDMA, special K, GHB, roofies)

Part 2 of Client Questionnaire (PRQ)

This part asks whether you disagree or agree with these statements. Make a check mark in the appropriate blank.

	Strongly Disagree	Disagree	Agree	Strongly Agree	FOR FACILITATOR USE ONLY
1. My use of alcohol or other drugs has caused many problems in my life.	_____	_____	_____	_____	☐
2. I can quit using alcohol or other drugs on my own.	_____	_____	_____	_____	○
3. I am glad to be in counseling.	_____	_____	_____	_____	☐

continued on next page

2 of 4

Page 3 of 4

••• CLIENT QUESTIONNAIRE •••

	Strongly Disagree	Disagree	Agree	Strongly Agree	FOR FACILITATOR USE ONLY
4. My problems are caused by alcohol or other drugs.	_____	_____	_____	_____	☐
5. I believe I am chemically dependent.	_____	_____	_____	_____	☐
6. My use of alcohol or other drugs has hurt others.	_____	_____	_____	_____	☐
7. I want to change my life and get away from alcohol and other drugs.	_____	_____	_____	_____	☐
8. There are many good reasons for me to stop using alcohol or other drugs.	_____	_____	_____	_____	☐
9. I know why people are so upset about my alcohol or other drug use.	_____	_____	_____	_____	☐
10. I need help for my chemical problems.	_____	_____	_____	_____	☐
11. Using alcohol or other drugs is a real problem in my life.	_____	_____	_____	_____	☐
12. I can control my alcohol or other drug use.	_____	_____	_____	_____	○
13. I have a bad alcohol or other drug problem.	_____	_____	_____	_____	☐

continued on next page

3 of 4

Page 4 of 4

••• CLIENT QUESTIONNAIRE •••

	Strongly Disagree	Disagree	Agree	Strongly Agree	FOR FACILITATOR USE ONLY
14. It will be a struggle for me to stop using alcohol or other drugs.	_____	_____	_____	_____	☐
15. It's okay for me to use alcohol or other drugs now and then.	_____	_____	_____	_____	○
16. I need to stop using alcohol or other drugs completely.	_____	_____	_____	_____	☐
17. I have more important things to do than to go to counseling.	_____	_____	_____	_____	○
18. I need help to stop using alcohol or other drugs.	_____	_____	_____	_____	☐
19. I am willing to give up my old friends so I can stop using drugs or drinking.	_____	_____	_____	_____	☐
20. I was forced into coming to counseling.	_____	_____	_____	_____	○
21. I think some type of intervention is a good thing for me.	_____	_____	_____	_____	☐

4 of 4

Scoring Part 2 of the Client Questionnaire

STEP 1: Assign these values to all the questions with a BOX ☐ in the column:

> Strongly Disagree = 1
>
> Disagree = 2
>
> Agree = 3
>
> Strongly Agree = 4

STEP 2: Add the scores in the BOXES = PRQ1
(questions 1, 3, 4, 5, 6, 7, 8, 9, 10, 11, 13, 14, 16, 18, 19, and 21)

STEP 3: Reverse the scores above and assign these values to the five questions with a CIRCLE ◯ in the column:

> Strongly Disagree = 4
>
> Disagree = 3
>
> Agree = 2
>
> Strongly Agree = 1

STEP 4: Add the scores in the CIRCLES = PRQ2
(questions 2, 12, 15, 17, and 20)

STEP 5: Add PRQ1 + PRQ2 = PRQ Score

INTERPRETATION GUIDELINES:

Low degree of willingness to change: PRQ Score = 21–39

Moderate degree of willingness to change: PRQ Score = 40–59

High degree of willingness to change: PRQ Score = 60+

Note: The results of the questionnaire should not be discussed with the client until later in the session, after the Triggers and Cravings Worksheet is completed.

STEP 3:

Administer the Pros and Cons Worksheet (10 MINUTES)

To move the first session from an introductory orientation to a more focused session, the pros and cons exercise is applied. This exercise is an exploration and discussion regarding the perceived positive experiences and negative consequences of the adolescent's substance usage.

1. Explore with the client the balance between the pros and cons of alcohol or other drug use in order to motivate the adolescent to consider a decision to change his or her behavior.

2. Utilize the Pros and Cons Worksheet to explore and discuss with the client the positive and negative consequences of the adolescent's substance usage. The answers to the questions asked in this exercise are to be recorded by the therapist on the Pros and Cons Worksheet. For the facilitator's convenience, a sample of this worksheet is shown below.

Sample of Pros and Cons Worksheet

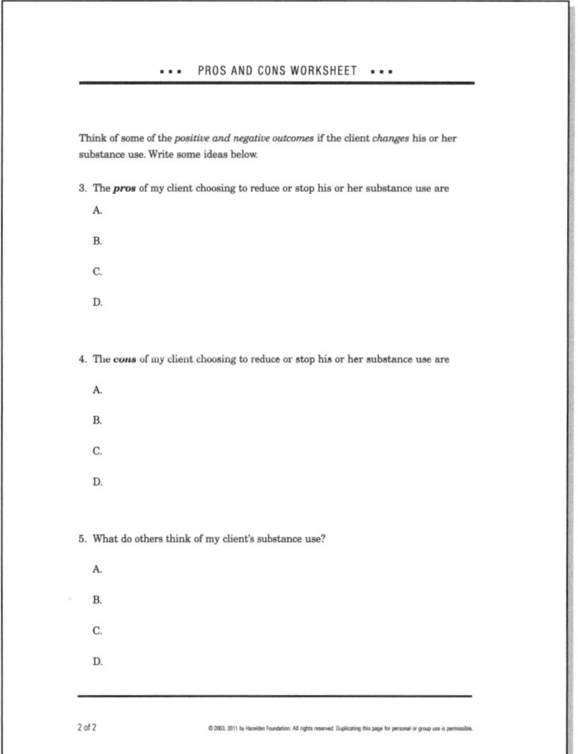

3. Ask questions similar to the following to help facilitate conversation with your client about question 1, the pros of using. Then, summarize the answers provided by the client, clarify any inconsistencies, and record the client's responses in the appropriate space on the worksheet.

"What do you like about using alcohol or other drugs?"

"What are the good things about using? What else?" (Ask repeatedly until the client has no more answers to provide.)

"Which positive effects of alcohol or other drugs matter the most to you?"

4. Ask questions similar to the following to help facilitate conversation with your client about question 2, the cons of using. Then, summarize the answers provided by the client, clarify any inconsistencies, and record the client's responses in the appropriate space on the worksheet.

"What don't you like as much about using alcohol or other drugs?"

"What are the not-so-good things about using? What else?" (Ask repeatedly until the client has no more answers to provide.)

"Which negative effects of using alcohol or other drugs matter the most to you?"

5. Explore your client's willingness to change his or her use patterns. Asking the adolescent to think about his or her future can be difficult. The objective here is to help the young person imagine the future if use did not continue. A change in the non-use direction may result in reduced penalties, consequences, and hassles from family and friends. The adolescent may gain back some privileges and freedoms that have been taken away as a consequence of his or her substance-use behavior. Explain that he or she can shed the reputation of a "druggie," "drunk," or "loser" and that the change will increase his or her self-respect.

6. Ask questions similar to the following to help facilitate conversation with your client about questions 3 and 4, the positive outcomes and negative outcomes of the client's choice to continue using. Then, summarize the answers provided by the client, clarify any inconsistencies, and record the client's responses in the appropriate space on the worksheet.

"What benefits are there to reducing your use of alcohol or other drugs?"

"What do you think would be the good things that would happen if you stopped using so much?"

"What do you think will happen if you continue to use the same way?"

If your client leaves out the major consequences if use were to continue, ask,

"May I tell you some of my own concerns as well?"

7. If the answer is yes, discuss possible consequences that the client may face or has faced based on what you have learned from prior discussions. Consequences might be getting arrested for a DUI/DWI, losing one's driver's license until age twenty-one, getting in trouble at school, or being placed on probation.

If the client leaves out some major benefits associated with discontinuing or reducing use, ask,

"May I suggest one or two more?"

8. If the answer is yes, organize your discussion around benefits that might occur based on prior discussions. For example, the benefits of discontinuing use may be to regain privileges or regain respect from his or her parents.

9. If needed, ask these questions to help facilitate conversation with your
    client about the pros and cons of using.

> "What do your friends think about your using?"
>
> "How does this affect your decisions about using?"
>
> "What do your parents think about your using?"
>
> "How do their attitudes affect your decisions about using?"

STEP 4:

Administer the Triggers and Cravings Worksheet (10 MINUTES)

This worksheet will help the adolescent cope with cravings and triggers.
As the adolescent begins to make a change, there will be difficulties along
the way. These blockades to abstinence occur most frequently during the
beginning stages of change. However, these obstacles can last for extended
periods of time over the course of change. It is important that the adolescent
understand that continued feelings of craving to use alcohol or other drugs
may be a normal part of the change process and that there are specific
strategies for coping with these situations.

It is important for the young person to discover what may trigger continued
drug use. Then the client is encouraged to learn skills for how to deal with
these situations with non-drug-use responses. The goal of this activity is
to encourage the adolescent to engage in rewarding activities that do not
promote or activate drug-use behaviors.

1. Review possible drug-involvement triggers with the young person.
    Young people often cite the following list of triggers:

    - contact with the drug

    - watching others use

    - situations where others are using, such as at a party

    - certain emotions, such as anger, frustration, boredom, and even
      excitement

    - physical symptoms—not feeling well; feeling nervous or tense

2. Review page 1 of the Triggers and Cravings Worksheet and circle the ones your client identifies as possible triggers for himself or herself. For the facilitator's convenience, a sample of this worksheet is shown below.

3. Ask the client,

   "Can you think of any other reasons for your alcohol or other drug use? Please tell me about them."

4. Write his or her responses on the appropriate blanks on the worksheet.

5. Select and read the scenarios on page 2 of the Triggers and Cravings Worksheet that seem to pertain most to your client. If time allows, review all four scenarios. Have the client respond to the questions for each appropriate scenario.

6. Summarize and record his or her answers on the worksheet.

Sample of Triggers and Cravings Worksheet

teen**intervene**

• • • TRIGGERS AND CRAVINGS WORKSHEET • • •

NAME / ID: _______________________________   DATE: _______________

Circle the reason or reasons for your client's drug or alcohol use.

- **Escape:** to avoid uncomfortable situations, arguments, memories, or actual physical pain. Some people want to escape from their pain and use drugs and/or alcohol to make themselves feel numb or to forget.

- **Relaxation:** to unwind and reduce tension. Some people do not know how to relax without using drugs.

- **Socialization:** involves social settings such as a party or family gathering. Many people who are shy or uncomfortable in these situations use alcohol and/or other drugs to help reduce uncomfortable feelings in themselves and to help relax in this type of situation.

- **Improved self-image:** to make one feel like he or she looks better in his or her own eyes.

- **Romance:** when someone is bored or unhappy with his or her life and feels he or she needs excitement or wants the feeling of being in love.

- **Frustration:** when a person has just given up trying to reach any worthwhile goal. This is a person who feels that nothing matters, and there is no reason for trying.

- **No control:** a person who gives up trying to control himself or herself. People who feel like this think they just do not want to make any more effort to fight the urge to drink or use other drugs.

- **Other:** please describe: _______________________________

____

Alternative suggestions: _______________________________

____

continued on next page

Worksheet adapted from U.S. Department of Health and Human Services, National Institutes of Health, National Institute on Alcohol Abuse and Alcoholism, *Cognitive-behavioral coping skills therapy manual.* Project MATCH Series, vol. 3. NIH publication number 94-3724.

© 2003, 2011 by Hazelden Foundation. All rights reserved. Duplicating this page for personal or group use is permissible.   1 of 2

• • • TRIGGERS AND CRAVINGS WORKSHEET • • •

1. You are standing in your kitchen, and you are watching your parent take a beer out of the refrigerator. In the past, you have taken one secretly for yourself. This time you don't want to. What do you do?

____

____

____

2. You are at a party with your friends, and someone passes you a joint. You don't feel like smoking it just now. What can you do?

____

____

____

3. You have had a really hard day. You got an F on your test, your best friend has turned on you, and you are really frustrated. What can you do instead of using drugs and/or alcohol?

____

____

____

4. You have a big presentation in front of the entire school tomorrow. You are really nervous and are having a hard time falling asleep. What do you do?

____

____

____

2 of 2   © 2003, 2011 by Hazelden Foundation. All rights reserved. Duplicating this page for personal or group use is permissible.

Worksheet adapted from U.S. Department of Health and Human Services, National Institutes of Health, National Institute on Alcohol Abuse and Alcoholism, *Cognitive-behavioral coping skills therapy manual.* Project MATCH Series, vol. 3. NIH publication number 94-3724.

STEP 5:

Give Feedback from the Client Questionnaire, Part 2
(10 MINUTES)

Now that you have discussed the pros and cons of drug use with your client, along with triggers and cravings, it is time to return to the initial Client Questionnaire. The process of motivating and enhancing client change continues with the activity in which the results from the intake assessment data are reviewed with the client. Personalized feedback is one of the key elements in helping the adolescent to change his or her drug-using behavior. Not only does this process help to organize and summarize the information that the adolescent has provided, the individualized approach helps facilitate the identification of personalized goals.

1. Prepare to discuss the results of part 2 (PRQ) of the Client Questionnaire. If you have not scored part 2, it is important to do so now.

2. Let the client know you would like to provide feedback. You might say,

   "I would like to go over the results of the questionnaire that you took. Is that okay?"

   If the answer is no, ask why and explore concerns.

3. If the answer is yes, show the questionnaire to the participant. Here is a suggested script.

   "We are going to review your responses to the questionnaire. I'll explain all this in detail. Please feel free to ask questions and make comments as we go along."

4. Solicit the participant's reactions as you review a sample of the client's answers. It is suggested that you review the answers to these items: 1, 7, 10, 12, 18, and 19. Provide information by discussing the meaning of the client's score or findings. For example, for item 1 you might say,

   "The answer you gave to this item (read answer) indicates that you have experienced many consequences and problems due to your use. Can you tell me more about this? What do you think about this?"

5. The total score of part 2 provides an indication of the client's willingness
    to change. Below are guidelines for how to discuss this.

"The results of part 2 of the questionnaire show a score that
indicates a *(low or moderate or high)* level of interest in getting
help with your drinking/drug use. How do you feel about this?"

If score is low: "What are some of the reasons you do not
want to change your drinking/drug use pattern?"

If moderate or high: "This is great. What are some of the reasons
why you are thinking about changing your drinking/drug use
pattern?"

6. Deal with resistance sensitively. Use empathy and reflective listening
    skills. Avoid pejorative phrases, such as "you are addicted." After you
    have provided feedback to the client, you may want to ask additional
    questions to further the discussion of the results. Below are a number of
    questions you could ask to continue the feedback discussion.

"What do you think of all of this?"

"Is there any part you have questions about?"

"What was most surprising to you? Which part concerned you
the most?"

"Do you see how your pattern of use places you at risk for
more problems?"

"Can you tell me more about your use of alcohol and other drugs?"

"How old were you when you started to use?"

"Was there anything going on in your life when you started to
increase your use?"

"What kinds of trouble, if any, have you gotten into because of
your use of alcohol or other drugs?"

STEP 6:

Administer the Ready to Change Worksheet 1   (5 MINUTES)

The session has progressed to the point where it is time to take a "temperature reading" of the client's willingness to change.

1. Say to your client something like this:

"Let's see how you feel about changing at this time. We've reviewed the pros and cons of using, triggers and cravings, and what changing your use pattern would mean to you. We have also reviewed the results of your questionnaire. Let's explore how ready you feel to change at this time."

2. Ask the client how ready he or she is on a scale of 1 to 10 to change use of drugs or alcohol.

"On a scale of 1 to 10, with 1 meaning 'not ready at all' and 10 meaning 'very ready,' how do you feel about changing your use of alcohol or other drugs? You can assign yourself any number from 1 to 10."

3. Record your client's answer on the Ready to Change Worksheet 1. For the facilitator's convenience, a sample of this worksheet follows on page 31.

4. Read the five statements at the bottom of the worksheet to the client.

"I will read five statements to you. Indicate which one best describes you."

5. Circle your client's response.

Sample of Ready to Change Worksheet 1

teen**intervene**

• • •   READY TO CHANGE WORKSHEET 1   • • •

NAME / ID: _______________________________   DATE: _______________

Here is a scale that will help you to determine how ready your client is to change his or her use of alcohol or other drugs. Circle a number on the scale that indicates how your client feels about this right now.

1   2   3   4   5   6   7   8   9   10

NOT READY   SOMEWHAT READY   VERY READY

Your client marked a ___________ .

This means your client is ______________ ready to change.

Please circle one of the following statements that best describes your client right now.

1. "I don't want to quit or cut down my use of drugs and/or alcohol."

2. "I don't really like to use drugs and/or alcohol, but I don't want to stop or cut down right now."

3. "I am thinking about stopping my use of drugs and/or alcohol."

4. "I have definitely decided that I want to stop using drugs and/or alcohol."

5. "I have already stopped using drugs and/or alcohol."

STEP 7:

Administer the Establish Goals Worksheet   (10 MINUTES)

The last significant task for adolescent session 1 focuses on assisting the client to establish goals. Given the nonjudgmental philosophy of *Teen-Intervene,* the counselor is encouraged to support any positive changes to which the client is willing to agree. Perhaps the goal will be as minimal as "to think about reducing drug use in the future." Admittedly, this goal may seem like a small gain to most, but it is important to begin the change process somewhere with a client. It comes as no surprise for professionals who have worked with many drug-abusing youth in treatment that most teenage clients do not readily choose abstinence as an immediate treatment goal. Risk reduction, use reduction, and normalization of use are meaningful improvements for the short term. Abstinence can still be a logical long-term goal, even when attaining this is preceded by nonabstinence goals.

1. Begin a discussion for the three questions on the Establish Goals Worksheet by asking your client the following:

   "How would you like things to be different?"

   "What do you think has to change?"

   "What's our next step?"

2. Elicit what the youth would like to change about his or her substance-using behaviors. Reflect responses and generate clearly specified goals. Identify people who might be helpful in supporting the youth's goals.

3. Reinforce your client's statements about goals with comments such as

   "That's safe."

   "That would be less risky."

   "Using alcohol or other drugs is not essential for fun."

4. Help the client consider the following possible goals:

   - self-monitoring (for the most recalcitrant client); have the client keep track of an aspect of his or her substance-use behavior that occurs frequently

   - abstinence

   - minimizing usage

   - risk/harm reduction

5. Also consider goals that are related to addressing the "functional value" of the client's substance use, which you can identify from the responses to the pros list on the Pros and Cons Worksheet. Examples: using drugs to feel more socially comfortable; using because of boredom; using to enhance fun with friends.

6. Record the client's statement about goals on the worksheet. If the client cannot come up with any goals, try this exercise again in adolescent session 2. For the facilitator's convenience, a sample of this worksheet follows on page 33.

Sample of Establish Goals Worksheet

teen**intervene**

• • • **ESTABLISH GOALS WORKSHEET** • • •

NAME/ID: _______________________________   DATE: _____________

In the space below, write down goals regarding your client's drug or alcohol use
that he or she will work on during the next seven to ten days.

1.

2.

3.

4.

What might get in the client's way of trying to reach these goals?

1.

2.

3.

4.

Where does this leave us now? What can your client do to prevent these obstacles?

1.

2.

3.

4.

STEP 8:

Administer the What Sets Off Your Alcohol and/or Other Drug Use? Worksheet (5 MINUTES)

Of course, your client is likely to face obstacles while trying to achieve his or
her goals. These obstacles may be barriers to your client's ability to change.
Support self-efficacy statements provided by the adolescent.

1. Consider this matter with your client by asking some of these questions:

"What might get in the way of you trying to reach these goals?"

"What might make it hard to actually change your substance-
using behaviors?"

"What do you need to do to achieve these goals?"

"Let's explore what kinds of feelings and situations set off your use of alcohol or other drugs. Can you identify three situations or feelings that seem to have led you to use?"

2. Record the client's responses on the appropriate blanks on the worksheet. If necessary, you may revisit the Triggers and Cravings Worksheet. For the facilitator's convenience, a sample of the What Sets Off Your Alcohol and/or Other Drug Use? Worksheet is shown below.

3. Discuss with the client how each goal may be faced with a barrier and review how to respond accordingly.

Sample of What Sets Off Your Alcohol and/or Other Drug Use? Worksheet

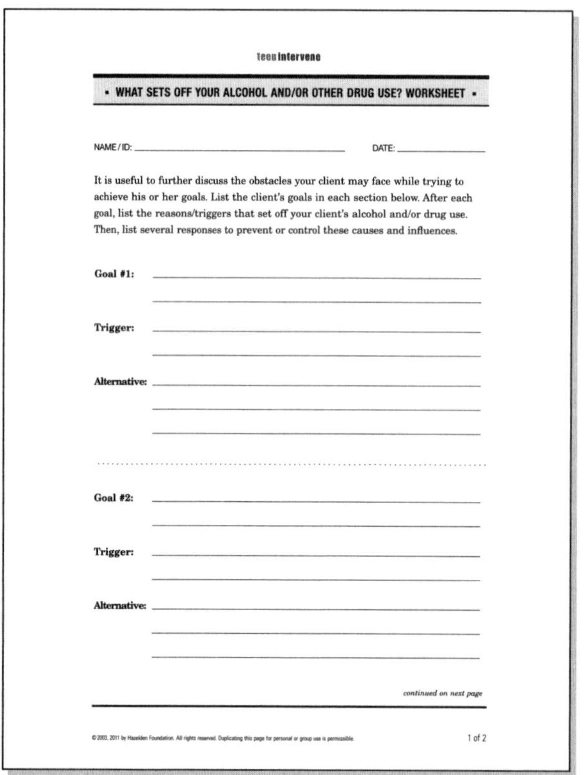

teen Intervene

• WHAT SETS OFF YOUR ALCOHOL AND/OR OTHER DRUG USE? WORKSHEET •

NAME / ID: _______________________   DATE: ___________

It is useful to further discuss the obstacles your client may face while trying to achieve his or her goals. List the client's goals in each section below. After each goal, list the reasons/triggers that set off your client's alcohol and/or drug use. Then, list several responses to prevent or control these causes and influences.

Goal #1: _______________________

Trigger: _______________________

Alternative: _______________________

Goal #2: _______________________

Trigger: _______________________

Alternative: _______________________

continued on next page

© 2003, 2011 by Hazelden Foundation. All rights reserved. Duplicating this page for personal or group use is permissible.   1 of 2

STEP 9:

Conclusion (5 MINUTES)

1. Review the worksheets from this session. Place an emphasis on the client's responses to the Establish Goals Worksheet and request that he or she work on these goals prior to adolescent session 2.

2. Ask the client whether he or she has any questions about the agreed-upon goals. Give the client a copy of Advantages of Not Using Drugs. For the facilitator's convenience, a sample of this handout is shown below.

Sample of Advantages of Not Using Drugs

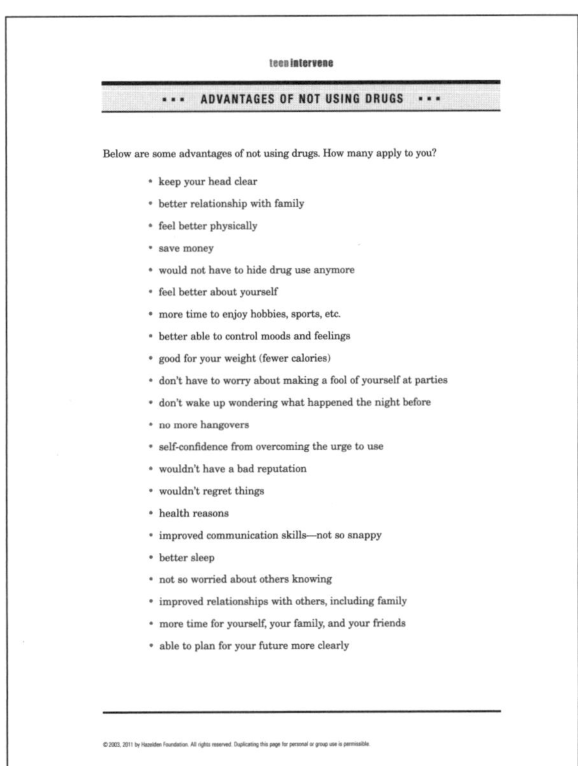

teen**intervene**

• • •   ADVANTAGES OF NOT USING DRUGS   • • •

Below are some advantages of not using drugs. How many apply to you?

- keep your head clear
- better relationship with family
- feel better physically
- save money
- would not have to hide drug use anymore
- feel better about yourself
- more time to enjoy hobbies, sports, etc.
- better able to control moods and feelings
- good for your weight (fewer calories)
- don't have to worry about making a fool of yourself at parties
- don't wake up wondering what happened the night before
- no more hangovers
- self-confidence from overcoming the urge to use
- wouldn't have a bad reputation
- wouldn't regret things
- health reasons
- improved communication skills—not so snappy
- better sleep
- not so worried about others knowing
- improved relationships with others, including family
- more time for yourself, your family, and your friends
- able to plan for your future more clearly

3. Save all the completed worksheets in a separate file for the client. You will need to review some of the worksheets before beginning adolescent session 2 and for a future booster session.

4. Set a date for session 2. A seven- to ten-day interval is recommended between sessions 1 and 2.

5. Thank the client for his or her participation.

ADOLESCENT SESSION 2

PART ③

INTRODUCTION

Welcome to adolescent session 2.

The purpose of session 2 is to further help the client evaluate his or her alcohol and/or other drug use and take steps toward the decision to quit using.

This second session consists of four steps:

- Review session 1.

- Review and administer the Ready to Change Worksheet 2.

- Acquiring new skills. The new skills will help your client deal with peer pressure, enhance decision-making skills, and reinforce social support systems.

- Conclusion.

This final adolescent session should be used to

- review progress made since the first session

- establish longer-term goals

- determine the need for a booster session in several months

Goals of This Session:

During this session, the client will

- acquire additional information from the *Teen-Intervene* program

- review session 1, including the Pros and Cons Worksheet and the Establish Goals Worksheet

- acquire new skills that will involve helping the client deal with peer pressure, enhance decision-making skills, and reinforce social support systems

- complete a second measure of the client's readiness for change

- establish longer-term goals

Time Required: 60–75 minutes

Materials Needed:

The following worksheets from session 1 and new ones for this session are located on the CD-ROM:

- completed worksheets from session 1: Pros and Cons Worksheet and Establish Goals Worksheet

- new worksheets for session 2: Ready to Change Worksheet 2 and Social Support Worksheet

Preparation Needed:

1. Read through this session so you are comfortable presenting it to the client.

2. Print and photocopy all the needed worksheets (one copy for use with each client).

3. Have available the Pros and Cons Worksheet and the Establish Goals Worksheet from session 1.

Background Information:

Establishing rapport with the participant is vital to the change process. Rapport building can be accomplished by

- employing the use of reflective listening skills

- being nonjudgmental

- asking questions to help investigate the positive and negative consequences of the substance-abusing behavior

The following is an outline for conducting session 2 in four steps. Instructions, helpful hints, and suggested time frames for each step are included, along with a suggested script.

Note: The therapist should fill out all worksheets in this session as he or she records the client's answers during the session.

SESSION OUTLINE

STEP 1:

Review Session 1   (30 MINUTES)

1. Review and discuss the Pros and Cons Worksheet from the first session with the client. See if the adolescent has shifted the "weight" of the pros and cons in favor of more cons relative to pros. If the client reduced use or abstained from use during the period between sessions, inquire as to what pros and cons were experienced by virtue of the reduced or non-use behaviors. Reinforce desired responses. Emphasize that any progress was due to the client's initiative.

2. Select questions from below to encourage discussion:

   "What was it like for you to use less (or not at all)?"

   "Did you think of any more advantages of not using?"

   "Did you think of any more disadvantages of continued use?"

3. Review the Establish Goals Worksheet from the first session with the client. Inquire about the client's progress with the goals set in adolescent session 1. Review whether the client's support system was a barrier or facilitator to the goals. Make suggestions when needed. Help the adolescent deal with any frustrations that he or she may have experienced while trying to make behavior changes. Remind him or her that sometimes change does not come quickly. Offer support to your client through continued application of helping techniques and strategies as discussed in session 1, and offer new ones as appropriate. Be supportive, positive, and nonjudgmental.

If the original goals appear to be too difficult or unattainable in the short run, then adjustments are in order. The therapist may even want to consider re-administering the Establish Goals Worksheet. Also, be alert for signs that the adolescent's problem with alcohol or other drugs may be worsening. If more assessment indicates greater severity compared to session 1, then consider the value of referring the client to a formal treatment program.

4. Select questions from below to encourage discussion:

   "Where do we stand with your goals?"

   "What did you do to help with achieving them?"

   "What got in the way, if anything?"

   "Where do you want to go next? Should we stay the course? Do you want to bring it up another level? Or should we step back and go slower?"

5. Consider helping the client with addressing and eliminating the barriers to achieving the goals.

STEP 2:

Review and Administer the Ready to Change Worksheet 2
(10 MINUTES)

1. Ask the client how ready he or she is on a scale of 1 to 10 to change use of alcohol or other drugs.

2. Record your client's answer on the Ready to Change Worksheet 2. For the facilitator's convenience, a sample of this worksheet follows on page 41.

3. Have your client read responses 1 through 5 and identify which one best describes himself or herself.

4. Circle your client's response.

5. Compare the score in this session with the score from session 1. If there is a higher score this time, reinforce this good news. Draw a connection between the improved readiness to change and progress that was made with the personal goals.

    If there is no score change, or a drop in score, provide support that drug use habits can be difficult to tackle and that it is okay if it takes some time.

Sample of Ready to Change Worksheet 2

teen**intervene**

• • • READY TO CHANGE WORKSHEET 2 • • •

NAME / ID: _______________________________   DATE: ______________

Is your client seriously thinking about changing his or her drug and/or alcohol use within the next six months?

YES   MAYBE   NO

Is your client seriously thinking about changing his or her drug and/or alcohol use within the next month?

YES   MAYBE   NO

Here is the same scale that you have seen before. This will help you determine how ready your client is now to change his or her use of drugs and/or alcohol. Circle a number on the scale that indicates how your client feels about this today.

1   2   3   4   5   6   7   8   9   10

NOT READY   SOMEWHAT READY   VERY READY

Your client marked a ___________ .

This means your client is ______________ ready to change.

Please circle one of the following statements that best describes your client right now.

1. "I don't want to quit or cut down my use of drugs and/or alcohol."
2. "I don't really like to use drugs and/or alcohol, but I don't want to stop or cut down right now."
3. "I am thinking about stopping my use of drugs and/or alcohol."
4. "I have definitely decided that I want to stop using drugs and/or alcohol."
5. "I have already stopped using drugs and/or alcohol."

STEP 3:

Acquiring New Skills (30 MINUTES)

At this point the client may benefit from additional exercises that promote the goals of the *Teen-Intervene* intervention and help the adolescent acquire the necessary skills to maintain a healthier lifestyle. Described below are three such exercises to help the client:

- Dealing with Peer Pressure

- Enhancing Decision-Making Skills

- Reinforcing Social Support Systems

Exercise 1: Dealing with Peer Pressure

1. Talk with the client about dealing with peer pressure, beyond the "just say no" approach. Many adolescents have a hard time refusing social pressures to use drugs without "losing face." Talk to the client about such peer pressures.

2. Have the client describe various situations in which he or she was pressured by peers or others to use alcohol or other drugs. Discuss how effective refusal techniques can be learned. Engage the client in considering how he or she might approach these social situations.

3. Introduce this exercise with the following script:

   "Learning how to say 'no' in different ways is always helpful. Tell me what you think about the following ways to refuse effectively."

4. Read each of the following examples and encourage your client to comment.* Try to identify which of the refusal statements your client will most likely use. You might record for the client the alternatives that he or she believes are most feasible. Discuss with him or her situations in which these statements will apply. Support him or her in trying one of these alternatives to "just saying no" the next time he or she feels pressured by someone to use alcohol or other drugs.

*List adapted from Centre for Addiction and Mental Health, Virtual Resource for the Addiction Treatment System, *A parent and community handbook.*

 "Say, 'Not now, I'm not ready.'"

"Just say, 'no thank you,' and leave it at that."

"Give a reason or excuse (for example, 'No thanks, I have a test/big game tomorrow')."

"Broken record—keep saying 'no' over and over again."

"Walk away—ignore the person and the situation."

"Avoid the situation—if you know there will be alcohol or other drugs at the party, don't go."

"Change the subject—start talking about something else."

"Strength in numbers—be with friends you can trust."

"Use humor—make a joke of the situation."

"Use your health as an excuse (for example, 'I'm allergic to smoke')."

"Reverse the pressure (for example, 'If you want a beer so badly, get one yourself')."

"Be honest and tell them you are not into it (for example, 'It's just not my thing')."

"Suggest an alternative—try doing something else."

5. Try role-playing a couple of refusal situations. Make certain that the adolescent understands that he or she must speak assertively and make eye contact while using these techniques. Reinforce that the client need not feel guilty or weak about a decision to refuse to use alcohol or other drugs.

Exercise 2: Enhancing Decision-Making Skills

Facilitate progress toward the therapy goals. The adolescent client may need help and support to enhance his or her decision-making skills. One of the ways to help is to teach him or her the following *five-step plan.* This plan may help sharpen the client's problem-solving skills when faced with personal triggers of substance use.

1. Guide the adolescent through real or hypothetical problems using the following five-step plan. You may use the opening script to initiate this exercise.

"Let's think about how people use effective skills to make good decisions when faced with unclear situations in life. To help you sort things out, here are five easy steps: stop, think, choose, act, and evaluate."

1. **"Stop!** Ask yourself, 'Do I really want to use in this situation?' Maybe you could do something other than drinking or using."

2. **"Think!** What are some ways you can decide to get out of using? List at least three."

3. **"Choose** one."

4. **"Act!** Do it."

5. **"Evaluate!** Ask yourself, 'How did it work?'"

"Following are two examples of a fictional situation in which a person could apply these five steps. I will read the first situation and then discuss with you how someone could use the five steps to make a good decision. After that, I'll read the second example. I would appreciate you working with me to figure out how to apply the five steps to that situation."

2. Read the following fictional situation.

"Your boyfriend/girlfriend's parents are going away for the weekend. He/she invites you over to hang out on Friday night. When you get there, you learn that many others have been invited as well. An older brother has bought a keg of beer, and many of your friends are already inside drinking. You decide to go in, and after your first beer, you start to have second thoughts. You don't want to lose your boyfriend/girlfriend. What could you do?"

3. Read and discuss the example below on how to apply the five steps to the situation above.

"First, **stop** and ask yourself, 'Do I really want to use or not?' **Think** of three alternatives to using, such as (1) ask my boyfriend/girlfriend to leave with me, (2) make an excuse not to drink, such as 'I have to work tomorrow,' or (3) put the glass down, go to another room, find someone to talk to who isn't drinking. Now **choose** one of the alternatives. Which one is most likely to work? Say you decide to leave the room. **Act** and do it. Go visit a nondrinking friend. Afterward, **evaluate.** How did this work?"

4. Read the second fictional situation below and encourage the client to discuss how he or she might apply the five steps to the situation.

"You are on the baseball team. A team member has been performing well above average lately and has quickly become the 'star player.' You ask your teammate how he/she improved so quickly. The teammate then shows you the new pills he/she has been taking to enhance his/her game. The teammate asks if you want to try some too. What could you do?"

5. Ask the client to apply the five-step plan to the situation above. Support your client in his or her efforts to use the plan. Teaching the adolescent to stop and think before acting helps reinforce his or her desire to choose healthier behaviors over using alcohol or other drugs.

Exercise 3: Reinforcing Social Support Systems

It is important for the adolescent to know that there are people in his or her life who will support his or her choice not to use alcohol or other drugs. You can help the adolescent recognize the supportive people in his or her environment.

1. Help prepare the client to fill out the Social Support Worksheet by first asking him or her the following questions:

    "Who among the people you know—friends, adults, whoever— will support your choice not to use alcohol or other drugs?"

    "What type of support would be most helpful for you?"

2. Share the examples below (in bold-face type) with the participant by asking him or her the following questions:

    "Is there someone you know who is good at coming up with ideas and alternatives to using substances?" (**Problem-solver**)

    "Is there someone you know who listens, is supportive, and is understanding?" (**Moral supporter**)

    "Is there someone you know who can help take off some of the pressure?" (**Load sharer**)

    "Is there someone you know who can answer questions and help you find other resources and information?" (**Information provider**)

    "Is there someone you know whom you can call for help if all else fails?" (**Emergency backup**)

3. Read the questions from the Social Support Worksheet. Discuss each one with the client and record his or her answer on the worksheet. For the facilitator's convenience, a sample of this handout follows on page 47.

Sample of Social Support Worksheet

teen**Intervene**

• • • SOCIAL SUPPORT WORKSHEET • • •

NAME / ID: _______________________________   DATE: _______________

Answer the following questions to the best of your ability.

1. Who may be able to offer my client support?

Suggestions:

- Think of people who have been helpful to the client in the past, such as friends, family members, or other people that he or she knows.

- Find people who are not biased, those who will not pick sides.

- If you can't think of people who can be of help to the client now, think of those who may be helpful later on.

2. Think of ways that these supportive people can help the client. List at least three.

continued on next page

Worksheet adapted from S. Sampl and R. Kadden, *Motivational enhancement therapy and cognitive behavioral therapy for adolescent cannabis users: 5 sessions.* Cannabis Youth Treatment Series, vol. 1. U.S. Department of Health and Human Services, Substance Abuse and Mental Health Services Administration, Center for Substance Abuse Treatment. DHHS publication no. (SMA) 01-3486.

     1 of 2

• • • SOCIAL SUPPORT WORKSHEET • • •

3. How can your client get the support he or she needs? List at least two examples.

4. List an example of the right time and place for your client to ask for someone's support.

5. Name someone who could use your client's support. Ask your client to tell you how he or she might help that person.

Worksheet adapted from S. Sampl and R. Kadden, *Motivational enhancement therapy and cognitive behavioral therapy for adolescent cannabis users: 5 sessions.* Cannabis Youth Treatment Series, vol. 1. U.S. Department of Health and Human Services, Substance Abuse and Mental Health Services Administration, Center for Substance Abuse Treatment. DHHS publication no. (SMA) 01-3486.

2 of 2

STEP 4:

Conclusion   (5 MINUTES)

1. Summarize the session. Emphasize the details of the client's goals for change. Review strategies to overcome barriers and encourage use of supports. Make sure to answer any questions. Congratulate the youth for maintaining commitment to the intervention.

2. Discuss the advantage of a booster session at some time in the future, such as in three months. This session can provide a useful review of progress. It is recommended that a booster session follow the structure of session 2.

3. Determine whether your client will benefit from referral information. This could be in the form of instructions to call the counselor in case of relapse. The client could also be given specific contact information for an appropriate program.

4. Thank the client for his or her respectful participation.

PARENT/GUARDIAN SESSION

PART ④

INTRODUCTION

Welcome to the parent/guardian session.

Parents/guardians may exert an enormous influence—either positive or negative—on their child's efforts to change substance-use behavior patterns. Research from the fields of family therapy and substance use prevention offers a set of basic principles that serve to facilitate or encourage healthy behaviors. These principles include

- adequate monitoring of the whereabouts of the adolescent

- consistent disciplining

- fostering a supportive interpersonal relationship with the adolescent

- exhibiting personal behavior that communicates a healthy relationship with legal substances

Part 4 describes a separate therapy session for use with the parents or guardians of the adolescent client who is receiving the brief intervention. The following is recommended:

- This sixty-minute session should be conducted after the two client sessions, about ten days after adolescent session 2.

- This third session would ideally conclude with a brief meeting with the adolescent and the parent(s)/guardian(s) to review everyone's short-term and long-term goals.

The purpose of the parent/guardian session is teaching and encouraging parenting behaviors that promote healthy change in their child.

Goals of This Session:

During this session, the client(s) will

- review the events that led their son or daughter to the brief intervention

- be introduced to the *Teen-Intervene* program

- discuss the topic of their alcohol and other drug use

- learn how to talk to kids about use of alcohol and other drugs

- review family rules about use of alcohol and other drugs, and determine the family's level of personal interest in helping their child change in a positive direction

Time Required: 60 minutes

Materials Needed:

The following worksheets and handouts are located on the CD-ROM (Spanish versions are also available):

- Parent/Guardian Worksheet

- Six Steps: Talking to Kids about Alcohol and Other Drugs

- Family Rules about Alcohol and Other Drug Use

- Parent/Guardian Questionnaire

- Parent/Guardian Goals Worksheet

Also on the CD-ROM is an article for parents/guardians called "Five Things Parents Can Do to Help Their Teen Avoid Alcohol and Other Drugs." You can offer this article to parents/guardians to read during or after the session.

Preparation Needed:

1. Read through this session so you are comfortable presenting it to the client.

2. Print and photocopy all worksheets and handouts to be used in this session.

Background Information:

Establishing rapport with the participant(s) at the outset of therapy is
vital to the change process. Rapport building can be accomplished by

- employing the use of reflective listening skills

- being nonjudgmental

- asking questions to help investigate the positive and negative
  consequences of the substance-abusing behavior

The following is an outline for conducting the parent/guardian session in
seven steps. Instructions, helpful hints, and suggested time frames for each
step are included, along with a suggested script.

SESSION OUTLINE

STEP 1:

Breaking the Ice   (10 MINUTES)

To begin your session with the parent(s)/guardian(s), we recommend the following:

1. Start with some casual conversation. Review the events that led their son or daughter to the *Teen-Intervene* program. Discuss their view of what happened and how they feel about him or her receiving therapy. Ask open-ended questions rather than yes/no or closed-ended questions. For example:

   "What do you hope your child will gain from the *Teen-Intervene* program?"

   "What has your son/daughter told you about his/her sessions from the prior weeks?"

   "What do you know about the goals your son/daughter has been working on?"

2. Give the parent(s)/guardian(s) an overview of *Teen-Intervene*. Explain the goals and methods of treatment. Summarize the main ideas. Answer any questions and address any concerns they may have. Be reassuring and empathetic in your answers. Below are statements you might use at this time:

   "I would like to review the goals and purpose of the *Teen-Intervene* program for your child. Please feel free to ask any questions or raise any concerns you may have."

   "The goal of the counseling is to collect personal information and then use that information to help an adolescent reduce or stop his/her use of alcohol and other drugs. Learning about the history of alcohol and other drug use can help us to individually focus the sessions."

"Each person has his/her own reason for using alcohol and other drugs. The *Teen-Intervene* program has been designed to meet these specific needs."

"With respect to your son/daughter, the long-range goal of counseling is abstinence. But in the short term, we are working on other goals as well."

"Do you have any questions or concerns?"

3. Provide a summary of the specific goals that are being addressed. Be general and stress that the goals are aimed at reduction of substance use and eventually abstinence.

4. This next exercise is optional. You may want to move the discussion to the topic of the parents'/ guardians' alcohol and other drug use. Naturally, this should not be a threatening line of questioning. The purpose of these questions is to determine if the parents'/guardians' use of alcohol or other drugs is unhealthy and, thus, will require personal change. Only discuss this topic if you are comfortable doing so. Here are some possible questions to ask:

"It may be useful to discuss your possible use of alcohol and/or other drugs."

"Did you drink alcohol when you were a teenager?"

"Do you currently drink alcohol? (If yes) Describe the circumstances in which you drink."

"What about your child's brothers and sisters? Do they drink alcohol? Do they use drugs?"

If the parent(s)/guardian(s) show signs of problems with their use, or problems elsewhere in the family, the therapist might say

"These issues look to be important to your son's/daughter's efforts to change his/her own use. We will return to this topic later in the session."

STEP 2:

Administer the Parent/Guardian Worksheet   (10 MINUTES)

1. Introduce this worksheet as the first of five forms used in the parent/ guardian session.

2. Begin with a general statement, such as this one:

   "There are a few specific questions that I would like to ask. These questions will help us discuss how you can help encourage and support your son's/daughter's goals."

3. Ask the six questions on the Parent/Guardian Worksheet and record the parents'/guardians' responses. For the facilitator's convenience, a sample of this worksheet is shown below.

Sample of Parent/Guardian Worksheet

teen**Intervene**

··· PARENT/GUARDIAN WORKSHEET ···

NAME / ID: _________________________________   DATE: _______________

"These first questions are about your family and especially your son/daughter. Be honest and feel free to ask any questions that you may have as we go along."

1. "Describe your family life. Is it warm and friendly? Do your family members get along? Or is there conflict among family members?"

2. "How would you describe your relationship with your son/daughter?"

3. "What types of things do you like to do with your son/daughter?"

4. "Let's turn to the situation with your son/daughter. What do you think are some factors that contributed to your son's/daughter's alcohol or other drug use?"

5. "Have you discussed with any friends or other family members what to do about your son's/daughter's use?"

6. "What steps, if any, have you taken already to try to prevent or reduce your son's/daughter's use?" (Reinforce positive steps.)

STEP 3:

Administer the Six Steps Worksheet   (10 MINUTES)

This worksheet will aid the parent(s)/guardian(s) in learning how to talk to kids about use of alcohol and other drugs.

For many parents, this topic is a very difficult one. Some parents choose to do nothing; others become upset by accidentally discovering some drug paraphernalia and then end up lecturing or berating their child about the dangers of drugs. Research has shown that parents are one of the most powerful influences on whether their child will use alcohol or other drugs.

1. Encourage parent(s)/guardian(s) to communicate that they disapprove of using alcohol or other drugs and would be very upset if use occurred. The following statements can be helpful.

   "Let's spend some time on the topic of how to talk to your son/daughter about use of alcohol or other drugs."

   "One effective and straightforward approach is to make sure you tell your child that you care about his/her well-being and that you are concerned that he/she not use alcohol or other drugs."

   "This approach uses a six-step process. Here are the six steps. Let's review each of these steps."

2. Give parent(s)/guardian(s) a personal copy of the Six Steps worksheet. Review each step with them. Answer any questions and address any concerns they may have. For the facilitator's convenience, a sample of the worksheet is shown on page 56.

Sample of Six Steps: Talking to Kids about Alcohol and Other Drugs

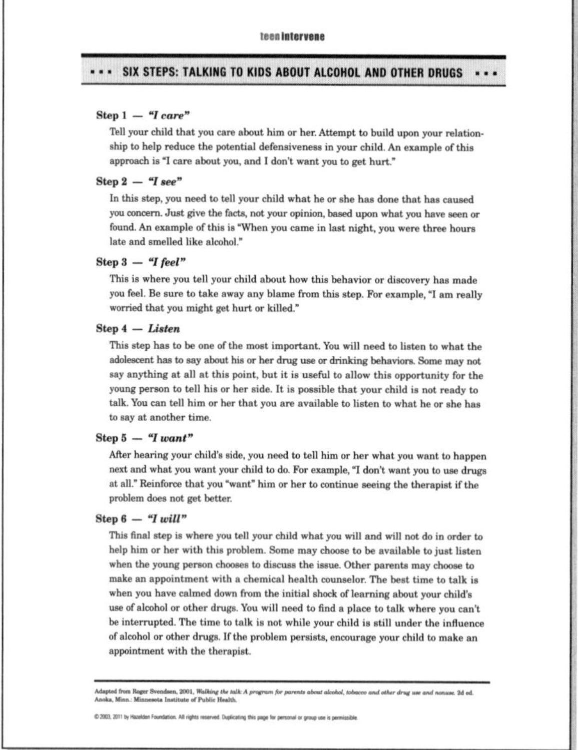

teen intervene

• • • SIX STEPS: TALKING TO KIDS ABOUT ALCOHOL AND OTHER DRUGS • • •

Step 1 — *"I care"*

Tell your child that you care about him or her. Attempt to build upon your relationship to help reduce the potential defensiveness in your child. An example of this approach is "I care about you, and I don't want you to get hurt."

Step 2 — *"I see"*

In this step, you need to tell your child what he or she has done that has caused you concern. Just give the facts, not your opinion, based upon what you have seen or found. An example of this is "When you came in last night, you were three hours late and smelled like alcohol."

Step 3 — *"I feel"*

This is where you tell your child about how this behavior or discovery has made you feel. Be sure to take away any blame from this step. For example, "I am really worried that you might get hurt or killed."

Step 4 — *Listen*

This step has to be one of the most important. You will need to listen to what the adolescent has to say about his or her drug use or drinking behaviors. Some may not say anything at all at this point, but it is useful to allow this opportunity for the young person to tell his or her side. It is possible that your child is not ready to talk. You can tell him or her that you are available to listen to what he or she has to say at another time.

Step 5 — *"I want"*

After hearing your child's side, you need to tell him or her what you want to happen next and what you want your child to do. For example, "I don't want you to use drugs at all." Reinforce that you "want" him or her to continue seeing the therapist if the problem does not get better.

Step 6 — *"I will"*

This final step is where you tell your child what you will and will not do in order to help him or her with this problem. Some may choose to be available to just listen when the young person chooses to discuss the issue. Other parents may choose to make an appointment with a chemical health counselor. The best time to talk is when you have calmed down from the initial shock of learning about your child's use of alcohol or other drugs. You will need to find a place to talk where you can't be interrupted. The time to talk is not while your child is still under the influence of alcohol or other drugs. If the problem persists, encourage your child to make an appointment with the therapist.

Adapted from Roger Svendsen, 2001, *Walking the talk: A program for parents about alcohol, tobacco and other drug use and nonuse.* 2d ed. Anoka, Minn.: Minnesota Institute of Public Health.

© 2003, 2011 by Hazelden Foundation. All rights reserved. Duplicating this page for personal or group use is permissible.

STEP 4:

Administer the Family Rules about Alcohol and Other Drug Use Worksheet   (10 MINUTES)

The purpose of the remainder of the parent/guardian session is to engage the parent(s)/guardian(s) in discussion about two issues: (1) family rules about alcohol and/or other drug use and (2) their level of personal interest in helping their child change in a positive direction.

1. Begin with an introduction of the Family Rules about Alcohol and Other Drug Use worksheet. (See sample on next page.) The therapist might say,

"I would like us to discuss the kinds of rules there are in your household regarding alcohol and other drugs."

2. Read aloud each item on the worksheet and have the parent(s)/guardian(s) privately complete the questionnaire or verbalize their responses while the therapist writes in the answers in the space provided.

3. Discuss their answers. Support responses that indicate healthy attitudes and behaviors in the family. Inquire for details when the answer is vague. Coach parent(s)/guardian(s) to offer answers that are more desirable.

4. Provide a copy of their answers and a worksheet for their own records.

Sample of Family Rules about Alcohol and Other Drug Use

teen intervene

• • • FAMILY RULES ABOUT ALCOHOL AND OTHER DRUG USE • • •

NAME / ID: _______________________________   DATE: _______________

1. Studies have shown that it can be helpful to include your child or children in creating your household rules. I have some questions for you regarding your family rules about using alcohol and other drugs. Do you have rules about this in your household? If so, would you be willing to share them with me?

2. If you were to have a family meeting, who do you think should be there? List the names of these people below. This list can include extended family members or others, such as a grandparent, aunt or uncle, neighbor, friend, priest or rabbi, counselor or therapist, or anyone else whom you think of as being helpful and supportive in the life of your family.

3. What family rules about alcohol and other drug use would you discuss?

Adapted from Roger Svendsen, 2001, *Walking the talk: A program for parents about alcohol, tobacco and other drug use and nonuse.* 2d ed. Anoka, Minn.: Minnesota Institute of Public Health.

STEP 5:

Administer the Parent/Guardian Questionnaire   (10 MINUTES)

This questionnaire explores the parents'/guardians' readiness to help their child change.

1. Introduce this questionnaire with a statement such as this one:

   "Next, I hope you will complete this questionnaire. It asks you about your attitude and expectations regarding your son's/ daughter's therapy. Let's discuss your answers when you are done. It shouldn't take long."

2. Give the parent(s)/guardian(s) the Parent/Guardian Questionnaire. This questionnaire (shown below) should be administered as a self-report form.

3. Review the parents'/guardians' answers to the questionnaire. (Hint: spend time reviewing the answers to these critical items: 5, 7, and 10.)

Sample of Parent/Guardian Questionnaire

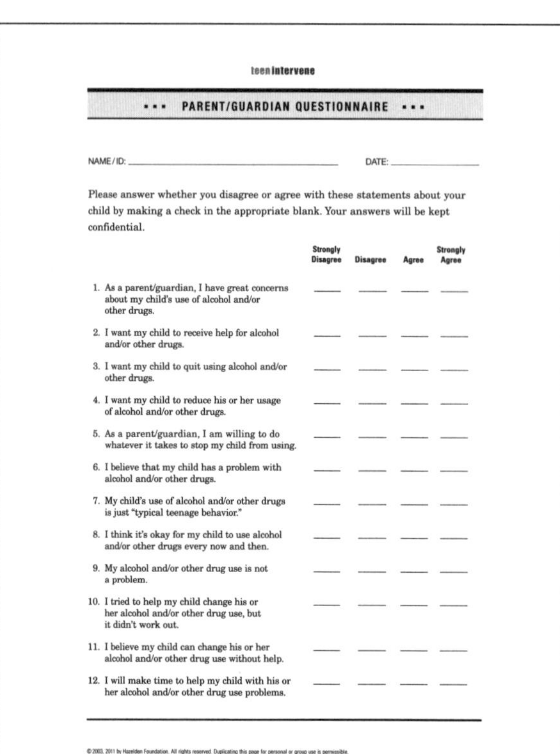

teen**intervene**

• • •   PARENT/GUARDIAN QUESTIONNAIRE   • • •

NAME / ID: _______________________________   DATE: _______________

Please answer whether you disagree or agree with these statements about your child by making a check in the appropriate blank. Your answers will be kept confidential.

	Strongly Disagree	Disagree	Agree	Strongly Agree
1. As a parent/guardian, I have great concerns about my child's use of alcohol and/or other drugs.	____	____	____	____
2. I want my child to receive help for alcohol and/or other drugs.	____	____	____	____
3. I want my child to quit using alcohol and/or other drugs.	____	____	____	____
4. I want my child to reduce his or her usage of alcohol and/or other drugs.	____	____	____	____
5. As a parent/guardian, I am willing to do whatever it takes to stop my child from using.	____	____	____	____
6. I believe that my child has a problem with alcohol and/or other drugs.	____	____	____	____
7. My child's use of alcohol and/or other drugs is just "typical teenage behavior."	____	____	____	____
8. I think it's okay for my child to use alcohol and/or other drugs every now and then.	____	____	____	____
9. My alcohol and/or other drug use is not a problem.	____	____	____	____
10. I tried to help my child change his or her alcohol and/or other drug use, but it didn't work out.	____	____	____	____
11. I believe my child can change his or her alcohol and/or other drug use without help.	____	____	____	____
12. I will make time to help my child with his or her alcohol and/or other drug use problems.	____	____	____	____

STEP 6:

Conclusion (5 MINUTES)

1. Review the intervention techniques discussed in this session. Discuss the therapy activities for parent(s)/guardian(s) by reviewing

   - parental discipline
   - positive and supportive behaviors (such as hugs, small talk, prosocial modeling of behavior, other social interactions not revolving around substances)
   - attitudes and behaviors regarding their own use of drugs

2. Reinforce what behaviors and attitudes the parent(s)/guardian(s) need to display more frequently (the positive actions) and the behaviors and attitudes the parent(s)/guardian(s) need to display less frequently (the negative actions).

3. Review the parents'/guardians' answers from the Family Rules about Alcohol and Other Drug Use worksheet and the Parent/Guardian Questionnaire.

4. Use the Parent/Guardian Goals Worksheet (shown on page 60) to record the specific behaviors, attitudes, and activities that have been discussed in this session and that you are encouraging the parent(s)/ guardian(s) to work on as support for the adolescent's goals. Give a copy of this worksheet to the parent(s)/guardian(s) for their reference.

Sample of Parent/Guardian Goals Worksheet

teen**intervene**

••• **PARENT/GUARDIAN GOALS WORKSHEET** •••

NAME / ID: _________________________________ DATE: ________________

Write down some of the goals for the parent/guardian to work on to support the child's goals.

1. ____
   ____
   ____
   ____

2. ____
   ____
   ____
   ____

3. ____
   ____
   ____
   ____

4. ____
   ____
   ____
   ____

STEP 7:

Closure and Combined Session   (5 MINUTES)

1. Use the last few minutes of the parent/guardian session to bring the adolescent and parent(s)/guardian(s) together to review the goals of each person. Discuss how each person will problem-solve if the adolescent's drug use escalates.

2. Agree on a plan for a possible booster session at a later point in time, such as in three months.

APPENDIXES

APPENDIX A

Select Adolescent Substance Abuse Screening Instruments

INSTRUMENT	DESCRIPTION	SOURCE OF INFORMATION
Adolescent Drinking Index (ADI)	This is a 24-item rating scale measuring the severity of drinking problems. It has been used with youths in schools and substance abuse programs, and with those under evaluation for psychological problems. It identifies those who need further evaluation and assists with treatment planning and recommendations. **Administration time:** 5 minutes **Scoring time:** 10 minutes **Training:** B.A. in psychology or related field and training in interpreting psychological tests.	Copyrighted **Contact:** Psychological Assessment Resources, Inc. (800) 331-8378 www.parinc.com **Self-administered:** paper
CRAFFT	CRAFFT is a brief test for screening for alcohol and other drug use in adolescents. It is a 6-item test based on a mnemonic of the individual items. Unlike some other screeners, the CRAFFT test screens for other drugs as well as for alcohol, and its questions were designed to be developmentally appropriate for teenagers. **Administration time:** 5 minutes **Scoring time:** 5 minutes **Training:** Requires no special training.	Public domain **Contact:** www.ceasar-boston.org /CRAFFT/index.php Interview or self-administered

continued on next page

  63

INSTRUMENT	DESCRIPTION	SOURCE OF INFORMATION
Drug Use Screening Inventory–Revised (DUSI-R)	Contains 159 true/false questions that measure problem severity in ten domains. It has been used with youth who have been referred for emotional and behavioral problems. It identifies treatment needs and provides a way to monitor treatment progress and aftercare. **Administration time:** 20 to 40 minutes **Scoring time:** 20 minutes, manual or computerized **Training:** Drug counselors and other qualified users; no special training required.	Copyrighted **Contact:** Dr. Steve Weatherbee eCenter Research Inc. (866) 480-2716 www.yourhealthcheck.org **Self-administered:** paper and computer Spanish version available
Global Appraisal of Individual Needs–Short Screener (GAIN–SS)	Contains 20 items that measure total severity and severity in each of the four main dimensions, with cut-off points for clinical decision making. Can be used in school, welfare, juvenile justice system settings, or within the general population. **Administration time:** 15 minutes **Scoring time:** 15 minutes **Training:** Minimal training required.	Copyrighted **Contact:** Chestnut Health Systems (309) 451-7700 www.chestnut.org/li/gain **Self-administered:** paper and computer

continued on next page

INSTRUMENT	DESCRIPTION	SOURCE OF INFORMATION
Personal Experience Screening Questionnaire (PESQ)	Contains 40 items that provide a problem severity score and overview of psychosocial problems, drug use, and faking tendencies. Can be used in schools, detention facilities, medical clinics, and settings where routine screening is needed. **Administration time:** 10 minutes **Scoring time:** 5 minutes **Training:** Instructions for hand scoring located in booklet. Can be used by wide range of health professionals.	Copyrighted **Contact:** Western Psychological Services (800) 648-8857 (310) 478-2061 www.wpspublish.com **Self-administered:** paper
Problem Oriented Screening Instrument for Teenagers (POSIT)	Contains 139 yes/no questions designed to identify problems and potential service needs in ten areas, with a follow-up questionnaire for measuring change in seven of the ten areas. Can be used in school, juvenile justice, medical, mental health, and substance disorder treatment settings. **Administration time:** 30 minutes **Scoring time:** 5 minutes by hand (computer scoring also available) **Training:** Requires no special training.	**For non-copyrighted version, see:** *Adolescent Assessment / Referral System manual available from:* ERIC (Education Resources Information Center) sponsored by the U.S. Department of Education www.eric.ed.gov **For copyrighted (computerized) version, contact:** PowerTrain, Inc. 8201 Corporate Drive Suite 1080 Landover, MD 20785 (301) 731-0900 **Self-administered:** paper and computer

continued on next page

INSTRUMENT	DESCRIPTION	SOURCE OF INFORMATION
Rutgers Alcohol Problem Index (RAPI)	Contains 18 items that assess adolescent problem drinking and related negative consequences. Advantages include ease of administration and usability with clinical and non-clinical populations. **Administration time:** 10 minutes **Scoring time:** 5 minutes **Training:** Requires no special training or credentials.	Not copyrighted **Contact:** Helen White, Ph.D. Erich Labouvie, Ph.D. Center of Alcohol Studies Rutgers University (732) 455-3579 http://alcoholstudies.rutgers.edu **Self-administered:** paper
Substance Abuse Subtle Screening Inventory, Adolescent Version (SASSI-A)	Contains 100 items designed to identify those with a high probability of having a substance use disorder. It includes subtle items to identify those who may be unwilling or unable to admit substance abuse. It has been used in criminal justice, employee assistance, and educational, mental health, medical, and vocational settings. **Administration time:** 15 minutes **Scoring time:** 10 minutes **Training:** Requires no special training. Free clinical consultation and technical support is available.	Copyrighted **Contact:** The SASSI Institute (800) 726-0526 www.sassi.com **Self-administered:** paper and computer

continued on next page

INSTRUMENT	DESCRIPTION	SOURCE OF INFORMATION
Teen Addiction Severity Index (T-ASI)	Contains 154 items that produce 70 ratings in seven domains. It is used in clinical settings with those with a substance use disorder, psychiatric, and co-occurring disorders to gather baseline information. **Administration time:** 20 to 45 minutes **Scoring time:** 10 minutes **Training:** Can be given by a trained technician or mental health professional.	Public domain **Contact:** Yifrah Kaminer, M.D. University of Connecticut Health Center (860) 679-4344 www.uchc.edu Semi-structured interview

Drug-Specific Information

The information in appendix B is adapted from *A Parent and Community Handbook* by the Centre for Addiction and Mental Health, Virtual Resource for the Addiction Treatment System; *Hallucinogens and Dissociative Drugs: Including LSD, PCP, Ketamine, Dextromethorphan* by the U.S. Department of Health and Human Services, National Institutes of Health, National Institute on Drug Abuse; *Tips for Teens: The Truth about Methamphetamine* by the U.S. Department of Health and Human Services, Substance Abuse and Mental Health Services Administration, National Clearinghouse for Alcohol and Drug Information; www.drugabuse.gov/parent-teacher.html; and www.drugfree.org.

When appropriate, the therapist can integrate this information into the adolescent and parent/guardian sessions.

ALCOHOL

Common Names

Beer, wine, brew, booze, hooch, moonshine, vino, sauce

What Is It?

Alcohol is a depressant that reduces the activities of the central nervous system. Alcohol is created by the fermentation of grains, vegetables, and/ or fruits.

Short-Term Effects

People abuse alcohol to become more relaxed, to become more sociable, and as an inexpensive way to get "high." Thinking becomes distorted, as do judgment, reaction time, and the decision-making process. Working or performing other physical and/or mental coordinated tasks will become difficult under the influence of alcohol. Mood may be affected as well as the ability to control one's temper and actions. Risk taking has been associated with alcohol use. When a person consumes a large amount of alcohol in a single occassion, it is called "binge drinking." The effects of alcohol can be increased if combined with other drugs. A "hangover" occurs when a person consumes a large amount of alcohol and feels ill the next day.

Long-Term Effects

The long-term effects of using alcohol can be very damaging. A person who consumes alcohol heavily on a regular basis may suffer from an inflamed stomach or pancreas, cirrhosis of the liver, cancers of the gastrointestinal tract, heart disease, high blood pressure, brain damage, and nerve damage. In the unborn babies of pregnant women who drink, the prenatal exposure to alcohol can cause fetal alcohol syndrome (FAS) or fetal alcohol effects (FAE). These include facial abnormalities, growth deficiencies, and damage to the central nervous system that can result in developmental delays, learning disabilities, hyperactivity, memory deficits, and behavioral disorders. Excessive use of alcohol can cause psychotic behavior and/or death.

Signs of Usage

Symptoms of a hangover include headache, stomachache, low blood sugar, dehydration, and possibly an irritation of the lining of the digestive system. An alcohol smell on the person's breath or clothing, as well as drunken behavior such as impaired coordination and slurred speech, indicates usage.

Legal Status

All states and the District of Columbia have a minimum drinking age of twenty-one years old.

CAFFEINE

What Is It?

The drug caffeine is derived from many plants including coffee, tea, cocoa, and some nuts. It is the most widely used drug in the world because caffeine is found in a number of commonly consumed foods and beverages like chocolate, coffee, tea, and soft drinks. The use of caffeine in energy drinks is increasingly popular.

Short-Term Effects

The short-term effects associated with caffeine intake are initially an elevation in one's mood. It reduces drowsiness and fatigue, while larger doses can cause irritability, restlessness, nervousness, and insomnia. Caffeine constricts the blood vessels and increases one's heart rate, blood pressure, production of gastric juices, birth defects in unborn babies, and urine output.

Long-Term Effects

The long-term effects associated with large doses include irritability, restlessness, nervousness, muscle twitches, rapid and/or irregular heartbeat, inexhaustibility, agitation, and insomnia. Caffeine has been proven to be a highly addictive substance.

Signs of Usage

Caffeine users may appear jittery, hyperactive, and talkative, as well as exhibit anxiety and withdrawal symptoms.

Legal Status

Caffeine is not a restricted drug. It is legal to purchase and consume, with the exception of athletes competing in certain events such as the Olympics (where it is considered a performance-enhancing drug).

CANNABIS

Common Names

Marijuana, dope, THC, pot, hemp, weed, ganja, grass, reefer, Mary Jane, hashish, hash, hash oil, chronic, gangster, boom

What Is It?

The drug comes from the cannabis plant. It appears as green, brown, or gray mixtures of dried, shredded leaves, stems, and seeds. Users may smoke it in a pipe or "bong" (water pipe), or rolled in cigarette or cigar papers into "joints" or "blunts." Forms of marijuana and hashish can also be inhaled as an odorless vapor in a battery-powered electronic cigarette or "e-cig." Hashish is a derivative of the plant material and is typically more potent than marijuana. Hash appears as a hard or soft resinous slabs that are broken up and smoked in a pipe, sometimes with added tobacco. Marijuana and hash can also be eaten, typically in baked goods. The active drug of these substances is THC (delta-9-tetrahydrocannabinol).

Short-Term Effects

Short-term effects are feelings of elation and relaxation, and possibly talkativeness. Fast pulse and higher blood pressure are possible. Use has been known to cause problems with short-term memory and concentration, relaxed inhibitions, disoriented behavior, and foggy thinking. It can cause confusion, restlessness, excitement, and even hallucinations.

Long-Term Effects

Long-term effects include possible cannabis use disorder. Loss of interest in formerly enjoyed activities and problems learning new things are also possible. A link has been established between chronic marijuana use and a weakened immune system. Users may develop chronic bronchitis, various forms of cancer, heart attack, stroke, and/or blood pressure difficulties.

Signs of Usage

Signs may include thirst or hunger (the "munchies"); red, bloodshot eyes; trouble with thinking, memory, and learning; loss of coordination; silliness or giddiness; sleepiness; dizziness; anxiety; and talkativeness.

Legal Status

By federal law, buying, selling, or possessing cannabis is illegal in the United States. But some states have legalized the medical use of marijuana to manage some side effects of cancer treatment and to treat health problems such as hepatitis, glaucoma, and depression. More recently, a small handful of states have legalized marijuana for recreational use; others have somewhat decriminalized it. For current information on state laws, check the Smart Approaches to Marijuana website at www.learnaboutsam.org.

COCAINE

Common Names

Crack, C, coke, flake, dust, blow, nose candy, rock, white lines

What Is It?

Cocaine is a fine white powder that is processed from the leaves of the coca plant. Typically it is snorted, but it can also be injected. Crack is a derivative of cocaine that is made by mixing cocaine with baking powder or baking soda and water to form a cake-like substance. This cake is broken down or cracked into small crystals about the size of a peanut. These small crystals are then smoked (also called freebasing). Cocaine is a forceful drug that arouses the central nervous system. A cocaine "high" usually lasts for only five to twenty minutes, and each time the user needs more to obtain the high.

Short-Term Effects

The short-term effects of cocaine include a burst of energy and a decrease in one's appetite. The user may feel more alert, but this is just an effect of the drug and not a reality. There is a risk of stroke caused by an increase in one's heart rate and blood pressure. Strange behavior and violent acts have been connected with cocaine usage. Paranoid psychosis is possible, as are seizures and/or convulsions. Crack cocaine has been found to be instantly addictive. One use of cocaine and/or crack cocaine can cause a fatal heart attack. The risk of overdose is high.

Long-Term Effects

The long-term effects of using cocaine include the deterioration of the individual's nose tissues (from repeated snorting of the drug). Tolerance and dependency develop quickly, and there is a high risk of overdose. Users who inject the drug may contract HIV or other serious medical conditions. A paranoid psychosis may develop that can be irreversible and permanent.

Signs of Usage

A person's pupils may appear larger than normal, and the person on cocaine may exhibit mood swings and irritability, a carefree attitude, talkativeness, and euphoria.

Legal Status

The legal use of cocaine in the United States is for medical application only. After some medical procedures, such as rhinoplasty, doctors prescribe the drug to help reduce the pain of surgery. Possessing, purchasing, using, and selling cocaine is otherwise illegal.

ECSTASY (MDMA, METHYLENEDIOXYMETHAMPHETAMINE)

Common Names

E, XTC, Adam, the love drug, designer drug; also called a "club drug" because of the usage by those who attend nightclubs or parties called "raves"

What Is It?

Ecstasy, or methylenedioxymethamphetamine (MDMA), is a psychoactive drug with hallucinogenic and amphetamine-like effects. There is no approved medical usage for this drug at this time. Generally, it is taken orally in the form of a tablet or gelatin capsule. The powder form of Ecstasy can be snorted as well.

Short-Term Effects

The short-term effects from low to moderate doses include a mild intoxication, euphoria, and a sense of pleasure. People who have used the drug report feeling more connected with others as well as a lack of inhibition. Large doses of this drug increase the negative effects and may cause alterations in one's perceptions, thinking processes, and/or memory. The agony of Ecstasy is the severe risk of dehydration and hyperthermia. Deaths have been caused by the hazardous increase of the victims' body temperature. This happens more often at raves as users overexert themselves while dancing all night long. Using Ecstasy combined with other drugs and/or with alcohol increases the dangerous effects. Psychiatric problems may develop that can last from days to weeks and, in extreme cases, years.

Long-Term Effects

The long-term effects of using Ecstasy include severe depression and concentration difficulties. Damage to nerves and brain chemicals that causes permanent memory and learning disabilities has been documented. People who have used this drug frequently have noted weight loss, confusion, irritability, depression, paranoia, psychosis, and fatigue. Some reactions in certain people may be severe and unpredictable from only one usage.

Signs of Usage

Users may experience sweating, increased heart rate and blood pressure, increased sensitivity to touch, nausea, anxiety, panic attacks, blurred vision, jaw pain (from grinding teeth), insomnia, vomiting, paranoia, and convulsions.

Legal Status

Ecstasy is illegal to purchase, sell, or consume in the United States.

GHB (GAMMA HYDROXYBUTYRATE)

Common Names

The "date-rape" drug, liquid Ecstasy, liquid X, easy lay, "G"

What Is It?

GHB is created in the human body naturally in small quantities. When larger amounts are ingested (and combined with other drugs and/or alcohol), it is very dangerous. In the liquid form, GHB looks and smells like water with a salty taste. GHB can also be in white powder or capsule form. GHB has been used to increase one's sensuality and physical responsiveness. It acts by depressing the central nervous system.

Short-Term Effects

The short-term effects of using GHB can include slower breathing and heart rate. The dosage is difficult, and it is very easy to overdose. Large quantities of GHB can cause nausea, vomiting, dizziness, amnesia, and vertigo. Higher doses can place a person in a coma-like state. The heavy user has the risk of vomiting while sleeping and choking to death.

Long-Term Effects

The long-term effects of using GHB are unknown at this time. It has been noted to be an addictive substance that can cause physical dependence. Quitting suddenly can cause anxiety, insomnia, paranoia, and hallucinations. GHB overdoses can cause a reduced heart rate, a loss of consciousness, seizures, coma, and death.

Signs of Usage

Those with GHB in their systems may exhibit sleepiness, nausea, vomiting, dizziness, amnesia, vertigo, and oversensitivity to touch.

Legal Status

GHB is illegal to purchase, sell, or consume in the United States.

KETAMINE

Common Names

A "date-rape" drug, drug special, K, special K, vitamin K, baby food, kit kat, ketalar, ketaset, bump, cat Valium, jet, honey oil, super acid, purple, special la coke, green

What Is It?

Ketamine is an anesthetic and painkiller that is fast acting. It was designed for use in veterinary medicine and in other special medical procedures. This drug has been used like GHB to render an individual unable to fend off a sexual assault. Generally, ketamine is found in the liquid form but can also be in the form of a white pill or powder. The powder is frequently sneaked into someone's drink, injected, smoked, and/or snorted.

Short-Term Effects

The short-term effects of ketamine are experienced within ten minutes of ingesting the drug. Its effects vary with the quantity ingested. Vomiting and the prevention of pain typically occurs. When the user eats or drinks prior to taking ketamine, it increases the chance of choking on one's own vomit. Higher doses cause lack of coordination, babbling, temporary amnesia, and a reduction of the heartbeat. This means that less oxygen is getting to the brain and muscles in the person's body. Unconsciousness and death are possible from only one use. Tolerance can be developed with repeated usage.

Long-Term Effects

The long-term effects of ketamine are unknown at this time.

Signs of Usage

Being withdrawn, sleepiness, distraction, and confusion are common symptoms. A person may have perceptual distortions with regard to time and his or her body.

Legal Status

Ketamine is legal only for veterinarians and medical use prescribed by doctors. Purchasing, selling, or using this drug without the consent of a physician is illegal in the United States.

LSD (LYSERGIC ACID DIETHYLAMIDE)

Common Names

Acid, blotter, dots, microdots, window pane, sugar cubes, trips (the effect of using the drug is called "tripping")

What Is It?

LSD is an odorless, clear or white, water-soluble material that has been synthesized from lysergic acid (found in rye fungus). Effects of this drug can last from six to twelve hours. LSD starts out as a crystal-like substance that can be crushed into powder. In most cases, this powder is dissolved and diluted and then transferred to sheets of perforated paper (similar to quarter-inch postage stamps).

Short-Term Effects

The short-term effects of taking LSD begin within thirty to ninety minutes. Most of these trips can include both positive and negative experiences due to the intense hallucinations. The effects are highly unpredictable and may cause alterations in one's personality, mood, expectations, and surroundings. Users have experienced an increase in blood pressure and heart rate, dizziness, loss of appetite, dry mouth, sweating, nausea, numbness, and tremors. The most notable effects are on a person's emotions and sensory perceptions. Many users have experienced "bad trips," a nightmare-like state of anxiety, paranoia, and fear of insanity and/or death.

Long-Term Effects

Some people have reported psychosis and other psychological effects that can last long after the trip has ended. This can produce a long-lasting psychotic-like state that may include manic-depressive symptoms and/or episodes. These effects can last for years in those who have no other psychological predispositions. Some long-term users of LSD have reported "flashbacks." Physicians have labeled these flashbacks as hallucinogen persisting perception disorder, or continuous and recurring sensory distortions and hallucinations. At this time, there is no treatment available to assist with this problem; however, some medications can help to reduce the symptoms.

Signs of Usage

Some users may appear to be experiencing several emotions simultaneously. A person's senses may become distorted and highly sensitive to colors, smells, lights, and sounds. Pupils are dilated and the person may be giddy, silly, or laughing for no reason.

Legal Status

Possessing, purchasing, using, and selling LSD is illegal in the United States.

METHAMPHETAMINE

Common Names

Meth, speed, crank, crystal, tweak, ice, glass, uppers

What Is It?

Methamphetamine is a drug that is used to increase alertness and relieve fatigue. In most cases, it is found in the form of a pill or powder. The powder will appear coarse and has a yellowish tint. The user may snort, smoke, ingest orally, or inject the drug. Due to the ignitable, corrosive, and toxic nature of the chemicals used to make this drug, there is a high risk of fires and toxic fumes from making the drug.

Short-Term Effects

Much like cocaine, methamphetamine will give an instant feeling of euphoria, or "rush." It arouses the central nervous system by creating a false sense of energy. The user will have an increase in heart rate, blood pressure, and energy; blurred vision; restlessness; delusions; and risk of stroke; as well as feel a loss of coordination and experience mind and mood changes such as anxiety and depression. The initial euphoric state is typically followed by a severe "crash" once the effects wear off. From one usage, death can result from a stroke, and physical and psychological addiction may develop. There is a high risk of overdose.

Long-Term Effects

The long-term effects of using methamphetamine can include chronic fatigue, paranoia or delusional thoughts/thinking, and permanent psychological damage. Methamphetamine has been found to be as addictive as and more powerful than crack cocaine. Liver, kidney, brain, and lung damage have been found to be associated with methamphetamine usage. Withdrawal syndrome is common with apathy, long periods of sleep, irritability, and/or depression. Users can have irreversible damage to blood vessels in the brain and risk a heart attack and/or stroke.

Signs of Usage

Methamphetamine users can exhibit restlessness, nervousness, irritability, dizziness, confusion, lack of appetite and/or anorexia, increased sensitivity to sounds, paranoia, argumentativeness, dilated pupils, increase in blood pressure and pulse rate, and long periods without sleeping or eating.

Legal Status

Possessing, purchasing, using, and selling methamphetamine is illegal in the United States.

NICOTINE

Common Names

Cigarettes, smokes, sticks, butts, Bogarts, bogies, chew, snuff

What Is It?

Tobacco comes from the dried and crushed leaves of the tobacco plant. It is the second most popular drug in the world next to alcohol. The drug nicotine in tobacco is responsible for the short-term effects from smoking and the addiction it causes. Tobacco can be smoked in pipes or cigarettes, chewed, or snorted in the powder form. All of these forms are just as addictive.

Short-Term Effects

The short-term effects of using nicotine can include an increase in pulse and blood pressure. Stomach acids increase, and the person's skin may become cooler. Urine production is reduced. The amount of activity in a person's brain and nervous system will first increase and then slow back down. Appetite is decreased, and the person will be less able to perform energetic and physical activities.

Long-Term Effects

The negative long-term effects of using nicotine are significant. The blood vessels in the smoker's heart and brain will narrow or darken, causing shortness of breath and frequent coughing. Pneumonia, bronchitis, emphysema, and other lung infections are common. Cancer of many different forms, as well as stomach ulcers, may develop. The person's skin becomes rough, wrinkled, and dry, and it ages prematurely. A pregnant woman who smokes can cause the baby to be born prematurely or to have low birth weight. Women who smoke and take birth control pills have an increased risk of developing blood clots or having a heart attack or stroke.

Signs of Usage

Users may exhibit frequent coughing, smoke smell on clothing and hair, yellowish stain of fingers and teeth, possession of a lighter or other tobacco products, and decreased appetite.

Legal Status

The sale of tobacco products is illegal to people under the age of eighteen in the United States.

OPIATES (OPIOIDS, NARCOTICS)

Common Names

Heroin: junk, horse, smack, H, skag, shit, mud, black tar, dope
Methadone: meth
Morphine: M, morph, Miss Emma

What Is It?

The family of drugs derived from the opium poppy is commonly referred to as narcotics. Opiates include natural substances that come from the opium poppy flower as well as synthetic drugs such as meperidine (Demerol), codeine, and methadone. Doctors prescribe these drugs to help people who need relief from pain.

Short-Term Effects

The short-term effects of using opiates include stimulation in the brain while the central nervous system is depressed. Initially, there is a pleasurable feeling or rush, which is followed by the considerable slowing of one's thinking and reaction time. Outcomes of using opiates include restlessness, nausea, vomiting, dry mouth, warm feelings in the body, heavy feelings of extremities, lack of consciousness, slower breath rate, constricted pupils, depression, cold skin that is moist and blue in color, coma, convulsions, and death. The potential for overdose is very high.

Long-Term Effects

The long-term effects of using opiates include addiction, infections, a reduction in respiration, and overdose. Using dirty needles causes some infections. This can lead to contracting HIV and other serious illnesses. Drug dependency and severe withdrawal symptoms are common. Slow, shallow breathing, clammy skin, convulsions, coma, and/or death can be caused by an overdose of these types of drugs.

Signs of Usage

Signs include scars (called "tracks") from injections, constricted pupils, loss of appetite, sniffles, watery eyes, cough, nausea, drowsiness, and restlessness.

Legal Status

Medical doctors can prescribe opiates for specific medical conditions. However, the use, purchase, or sale of these drugs without a prescription is illegal in the United States.

PCP (PHENCYCLIDINE)

Common Names

Angel, angel dust, boat, dummy dust, love boat, peace, supergrass, zombie

What Is It?

PCP is classified as a dissociative anesthetic. It is a sedative that was available in pill form in the 1960s. Today it is found in a powder form that is often sprinkled on marijuana, tobacco, or other herbs and then smoked in cigarette form. It can also be snorted. PCP alters the neurotransmitters in the brain, causing a feeling of euphoria.

Short-Term Effects

The short-term effects of PCP include a feeling of having an "out-of-body" experience. PCP can cause shallow, rapid breathing, as well as an increase in heart rate, blood pressure, and body temperature. The user may feel dizzy, nauseous, and uncoordinated, and have blurred vision and/or hallucinations. The person can experience severe muscle contractions that can cause a bone fracture, kidney damage, or kidney failure. Higher doses can cause convulsions, coma, hyperthermia, violent episodes, and death.

Long-Term Effects

The long-term usage of PCP can cause addiction and withdrawal syndrome. Using this drug long term can cause memory loss, depression, disorientation, and suicidal tendencies.

Signs of Usage

Users of PCP may exhibit multiple and dramatic behavioral changes, dizziness, nausea, and a lack of coordination.

Legal Status

Possessing, purchasing, using, and selling PCP is illegal in the United States.

ROHYPNOL

Common Names

A "date-rape" drug, roofies, roachies, La Rocha, ruffies, ropes, pappas, ro-shays, robinal, the forget pill, pastas, peanuts

What Is It?

Rohypnol is the name brand for flunitrazepam. It is a benzodiazepine medicine that has sedative effects. Recently it has been given underhandedly by men to women to make them unable to defend themselves from a sexual assault. The tablet form is common. Since 1999, these tablets have been adjusted to dissolve slower, make clear beverages blue, and make dark beverages murky so it is easier to detect. When Rohypnol is combined with alcohol and/or other drugs, the increased effects can cause death.

Short-Term Effects

The short-term effects of using Rohypnol include drowsiness, feelings of relaxation, dizziness, confusion, and discoordination. The person may also become unconscious or black out for eight to twenty-four hours. Users may appear to be intoxicated or drunk. A reduction in one's inhibitions and judgment has been indicated. Some may use Rohypnol to increase sensuality and one's physical responsiveness. The effects of the drug usually are felt within the first thirty minutes. The peak is after about two hours and typically lasts for around eight hours.

Long-Term Effects

The long-term effects of using Rohypnol include physical dependency.

Signs of Usage

Those with Rohypnol in their systems may exhibit slurred speech, confusion, physical weakness, severe drowsiness, and difficulty in walking.

Legal Status

Rohypnol is illegal to purchase, sell, or consume in the United States.

SOLVENTS AND AEROSOLS/INHALANTS

Common Names

Gas, glue, sniff (the process of inhaling them is called "huffing")

What Is It?

Solvents and inhalants are found in many household products, such as gas in aerosol cans, correction fluid, spray paint, air freshener, glue, marking pens, gasoline, and model airplane glue. These substances were not designed to be used as drugs.

Short-Term Effects

The short-term effects of inhaling these chemicals include lightheadedness, euphoria, and sometimes a fantasy-like state. Nausea is common, and drooling can occur while under the influence of these chemicals. Sneezing and coughing can happen. A loss of muscular coordination, as well as a reduction of reflex speed, has been indicated. Permanent brain damage and death can occur from only one usage.

Long-Term Effects

Long-term effects such as weight loss, nosebleeds, bloodshot eyes, and sores on the nose and mouth are common. An interference with the growth of blood cells has been found to be connected with inhaling these chemicals. Suffocation and heart failure can cause permanent brain damage or death. Fatigue, mental confusion, depression, irritability, hostility, paranoia, and neurological damage may occur.

Signs of Usage

The user may become sensitive to light; have slurred speech, drowsiness, or loss of consciousness; have a runny nose and/or watery eyes; exhibit a loss of muscle control; and develop sores on the nose and mouth. Paint on the face and hands are another sign of usage.

Legal Status

Possessing these types of solvents, aerosols, and inhalants is legal in the United States. However, a person must be eighteen years old to purchase them in many states.

STEROIDS

Common Names

Oral: Anadrol, Oxandrin, Dianobol, Winstrol

Injected: Deca-Durabolin, Durabolin, Depo-Testosterone, and Equipoise.

The street name for dehydroepiandrosterone (DHEA) is Andro, which can be found in health food stores as a dietary supplement.

What Is It?

Anabolic steroids are synthetic compounds that are related to the male sex hormone testosterone. They come in either tablet or liquid forms and are taken orally or injected. Bodybuilders, weight lifters, wrestlers, and other athletes use them because they can facilitate skeletal muscle growth. These athletes claim that steroids enhance their athletic performance. Research has found that steroid use can be highly addictive.

Short-Term Effects

Steroids may contribute to an increase in body weight and muscular strength. Side effects include but are not limited to psychological reactions such as anger and aggressiveness. Physiological effects may include damage to the liver, heart attacks, acne, cysts, oily hair and skin, and a disruption of the normal production of hormones. In males, steroids can cause a low sperm count, a reduction of the testes, hair loss, male breasts, and more. In females, steroids can cause excessive body hair and loss of scalp hair, coarse skin, an enlarged clitoris, and a deepening of the voice. In adolescents, steroids can affect bone growth by signaling the bones to stop growing sooner than they should. This effect is irreversible.

Long-Term Effects

The risk for heart attacks and strokes prior to the age of thirty is significant. Some of the effects listed under Short-Term Effects are irreversible. Blood clots and liver tumors are possible. Withdrawal symptoms can cause depression, mood swings, fatigue, restlessness, loss of appetite, loss of sex drive, eating disorders, and other serious complications.

Signs of Usage

Some people who actively use anabolic steroids have shown signs of irritability and aggression.

Legal Status

Several forms of steroids can be found in health food stores under the guise of a dietary supplement (for example, DHEA or Andro—see above). Most others call for a prescription from a certified physician.

SYNTHETIC DRUGS: SYNTHETIC CANNABINOIDS

Common Names

Names include fake marijuana, K2, and Spice; often sold illegally in retail outlets or online as "herbal incense" or "potpourri." It is also known as Skunk, Yucatan Fire, Moon Rocks, and other names.

What Is It?

Synthetic cannabinoids are man-made chemicals that are applied (sometimes sprayed) onto plant material and falsely marketed as a "legal" high. Users claim that synthetic cannabinoids mimic the active ingredient in marijuana, THC. The drug appears as a brownish mixture of dried, shredded plant material, similar to marijuana. Mixtures vary; they may also contain other psychoactive plant materials. It may be sold commercially in foil or plastic packets; it is also sold on the street. It is typically smoked, sometimes mixed with marijuana, in cigarette (joint) form or in a pipe.

Short-Term Effects

Elevated mood, relaxation, altered perceptions; possibly agitation, anxiety, hallucinations.

Long-Term Effects

Effects may include addiction; severe anxiety; panic attacks; tremors, spasms, seizures; hallucinations, psychotic episodes, suicidal thoughts.

Signs of Usage

Red or bloodshot eyes, fast pulse, pale skin, nausea. Possible muscle spasms, panic attacks, psychotic episodes. Use is alarmingly high: in 2012, one in nine U.S. high school seniors reported using synthetic marijuana in the past year, placing it as their second most frequently used illegal drug (after marijuana). Source: NIDA, Monitoring the Future 2012 p. 14, www.monitoringthefuture.org/pubs/monographs/mtf-overview2012.pdf.

Legal Status

Throughout history, people have devised new psychoactive substances, often staying a step ahead of legal and social controls. Synthetic marijuana is among the latest in this category. It is widely available on the Internet, although recent laws have made it illegal or less available in retail outlets. It is often labeled "not for human consumption" to mask its intended purpose and avoid Food and Drug Administration regulatory oversight. The federal government has been working with state, local, and non-governmental partners to put policies and legislation in place to educate people about the tremendous health risk posed by synthetic drugs, and to combat their distribution.

SYNTHETIC DRUGS: SYNTHETIC SPEED

Common Names

Synthetic speed is often sold illegally in retail outlets as "bath salts," "jewelry cleaner," or "plant food." Online it may be marketed under names such as Ivory Wave, Bloom, Cloud Nine, Lunar Wave, Vanilla Sky, White Lightning, and Scarface.

What Is It?

Synthetic speed mimics the effects of amphetamines. These emerging drugs contain synthetic chemicals related to cathinone, an amphetamine-like stimulant. Because these compounds are made in clandestine labs, users have no way of knowing their contents, potency, or toxicity, adding to their danger. The drug typically appears as a white or brown crystalline powder, often sold in small plastic or foil packages. It can be taken orally, snorted, or injected.

Short-Term Effects

Euphoria; enhanced mood, sociability, and sex drive; confusion, headache, muscle tension, sweating, nausea, dizziness.

Long-Term Effects

Very high potential for addiction; long-term depression, aberrant behavior (due to a distortion of the brain's reward system), paranoia, delusions, suicidal thoughts..

Signs of Usage

Reduced need for food and sleep; sweating, nausea, cold or blue fingers; long-term signs may include depression, paranoia, strange behavior.

Legal Status

Throughout history, people have devised new psychoactive substances, often staying a step ahead of legal and social controls. Synthetic speed and synthetic cannabinoids are among the latest in this category, and more are sure to follow. Both are widely available on the Internet, although recent laws have made them illegal or less available in retail outlets. Both are often labeled "not for human consumption" to mask their intended purpose and avoid Food and Drug Administration regulatory oversight of the manufacturing process. The federal government has been working with state, local, and non-governmental partners to put policies and legislation in place to educate people about the tremendous health risk posed by these substances, and to combat their distribution

Frequently Asked Questions

Why Do Adolescents Use Alcohol and Other Drugs?

The reasons for adolescent drug use are mixed. There is no easy answer. There are several factors to consider, including physiological, psychological, and sociological influences. Physiological influences can be anything from a family history of alcoholism and/or substance abuse to mental health disorders. Psychological factors can include stress, inadequate social skills, negative affect, personality, and low self-image. Sociological influences can range from family and peer interactions to ethnic background, neighborhood, and religion. Below is a list of variables that research has shown are related to the onset and continuance of alcohol and other drug use (Clayton 1992).

- childhood exposure to alcohol and other drugs

- permissive family drinking or drug use customs and attitudes

- activities associated with drinking or other drug use

- social rewards for drinking and other drug use

Common behavioral characteristics may include

- impulsiveness

- aggressiveness

- gratification seeking

- low motivation for achievement

- psychopathology

Some additional theories support the idea that adolescents use substances because they are readily available as a quick and inexpensive method to make one feel good, to gain acceptance from peers, or to serve as a coping mechanism to relieve the symptoms of depression, tension, and pressure (Clark and Winters 2002). Environmental factors such as a stressful event (for example, death, illness, or injury) can also trigger this behavior. Segal and colleagues (1982) discovered three main objectives for substance use among adjudicated adolescents. These are

1. to expand awareness

2. to enjoy the drug effect (to get high)

3. to increase activity and satisfy curiosity

In sum, one cannot talk about the causes of adolescent substance use without touching upon the developmental transition of adolescence in general. Puberty, cognitive development, and identity development are a few of the hurdles that adolescents must face in their path toward adulthood. Increased health risks, including substance use disorders, are best understood in relation to this transitional period.

Who Is at Risk for Developing a Substance Use Disorder?

Deviations of temperament in early childhood have indicated a risk for a substance use disorder in later life (Galanter and Kleber 1999). The most common characteristics are externalizing and internalizing behaviors, irritability, impulsive behaviors, reduced attention span, aggressive behaviors, and excessively "emotional" reactions to minor events. Research has shown that there is a solid link between children diagnosed with a mental health disorder (for example, attention-deficit/hyperactivity disorder) and a substance use disorder.

Environmental factors also contribute to the development of a substance use disorder. Stressful events, lack of parental support and supervision, and deviant peer groups all play a supportive role. Social and cultural norms, socioeconomic factors, neighborhood, and lack of judicial enforcement can be included as risk factors.

Lawson, Peterson, and Lawson (1983) described four types of parenting styles related to the development of a substance use disorder. These styles are

- alcoholic parent(s)

- teetotaling (total abstinence)

- overdemanding

- overprotective

Peck (1983) stated that if adolescents have friends who use marijuana, 92 percent of those adolescents used as well. If only a few friends were users, 66 percent did not use marijuana. It makes sense that parents, guardians, teachers, and other people involved with these young people need to pay closer attention to daily activities and associated peers.

What Are the Differences between Mild, Moderate, and Severe Substance Use Disorders as Defined by *DSM-5*?

DSM-5 no longer uses the term "abuse" as a diagnostic term: instead, substance use disorders are classified as mild, moderate, or severe. As applied to adolescents, these distinctions are somewhat controversial. Some believe that any substance use by adolescents is highly problematic since, for example, alcohol is not legal for use until they have reached the legal drinking age. But *Teen-Intervene* acknowledges this spectrum of severity. It is designed for adolescents with mild to moderate substance use disorders: use that has progressed beyond the initial experimentation stages, is now more frequent, and has some negative consequences.

Under the *DSM-5*'s diagnostic system, substance use disorders are listed under the heading "Substance-Related and Addictive Disorders." The severity of each substance-related disorder—alcohol use, cannabis use, opioid use, and so on—is gauged by eleven criteria, listed in full in the *DSM-5*. Notably, craving has been added to this list of criteria, while legal involvement has been deleted: an appropriate change for adolescent diagnostics. The person who meets two or three of these eleven criteria has a mild disorder; four to five indicate a moderate disorder; six or more a severe disorder.

This terminology change helps remove the misleading implication that "abuse" always precedes "dependence," which is not always the case (e.g., some users show loss of control before they encounter negative social or personal consequences resulting from use). In general, however, severity is indicated by the extent to which the youth continues to seek out and use substances, regardless of the harsh personal consequences. For both adults and youth, a hallmark of severe substance use disorder is loss of control over use. Whereas most youths who abuse substances do not become dependent (Chung and Martin 2011), substance abuse is a significant health risk for young people.

Lawson and Lawson (1992) offer a list of signs to indicate drug abuse among adolescents. Some of these signs are

- a sudden change in the child's peer group
- experiencing significant highs and lows in his or her energy level and behavior
- a strong defiance toward rules and regulations
- excessive sleeping
- excessive excuses for misbehavior(s)
- poor hygiene
- self-isolation
- a drastic change in weight
- withdrawal from activities that were formerly enjoyed
- defensiveness
- coming home under the influence
- exhibiting a short fuse (lack of anger management skills)

A few of these can be viewed as typical adolescent behavior. However, it is important to recognize these signs as signals to pay closer attention to the adolescent and the changes in his or her behavior. Additional warning signs may include

- trouble in school (truancy, detentions, suspensions, and failing grades)
- poor social skills
- low self-esteem
- low self-efficacy

What Are Some Protective Factors to Prevent Substance Use Disorders?

Protective factors include people, activities, and skills that help prevent an adolescent from using alcohol or other drugs. The more protective factors an adolescent is exposed to, the more positive the outcome is likely to be. All people have the ability to lead a healthy lifestyle that does not include substance abuse. The young people who have a strong sense of self, a supportive family, and non-using peers generally have a decreased risk of developing a substance abuse problem. The following list details several protective factors for adolescents.

- participating in a Head Start program at an early age
- parents whose parenting style represents a more authoritative approach
- a peer group or best friend who does not use
- positive role models (for example, coaches, teachers, clergy, extended family)
- a positive self-image and self-esteem
- social skills training
- an affiliation with one's school (for example, band, team sports, clubs)
- academic competence and success
- having hobbies or other positive activities outside of school
- being resilient in cases of high risk, stress, or traumatic events

A resilient adolescent is one who can spring back in the face of adversity. Resiliency is a strength that supports the young adult in maintaining sobriety during difficult and often pressuring situations.

Why Use *Teen-Intervene*?

The use of brief intervention for substance abuse difficulties is not a new concept. Drug and alcohol counselors, psychologists, health care providers, and social workers have used this type of treatment with adults for years. In addition, a variety of other methods have proven effective in treating adolescents with substance use disorders. However, the cost factor often limits or prohibits these young adults from receiving the treatment that they desperately need. *Teen-Intervene* provides a cost-effective means to increase the availability of treatment.

Treatment time is very limited in *Teen-Intervene*. The intention is to reach the desired goal within two to three concise sessions. It is due to this factor that the sessions must be highly organized and structured. Because there are only a few sessions, attendance and dropout rates may be reduced with this form of treatment.

Teen-Intervene can be used to increase the desire and motivation to change, improve one's self-efficacy skills, teach about the harm associated with substance abuse, teach preventative coping skills, and reinforce and establish support systems. Alcohol and/or other drug abuse are associated with

- family violence

- high-risk sexual behavior

- sexual assaults

- prostitution

- robberies

- arrests/convictions

- physical assaults

- murders

- traffic fatalities

- drowning

- suicide

What Communication Strategies Are Important in the Parent/Guardian Session?

In working with parents/guardians, there are some things to keep in mind. First, this interview will be awkward, as there is no established relationship. The goal is to obtain information that can help to understand why their child is using substances. Make sure that parents/guardians understand this goal. Be clear and concise and try not to use technical terms or jargon. This is their time and should be used effectively. Make sure that you are meeting or telephoning at a convenient time. You may have to reschedule this meeting or telephone interview. Be patient and employ a variety of communication strategies. Most of all, thank them for their time and effort in this study. Here are a few additional things to keep in mind:

- Understand that some parents/guardians may not be able to read and write as well as their child.

- Be considerate.

- Be patient—some parents may take longer to complete the interview than others.
- Be understanding with regard to their individual circumstances.
- Don't place blame.
- Utilize reflective listening by reverbalizing what is said; for example, "I think I hear you saying . . ."
- Be cautious; some people may have strong feelings around this issue.
- Be nonjudgmental.
- Be nonlabeling.
- Be consistent.
- Watch your words—language in a conversation can either promote collaboration or end the dialogue.
- Recognize the value of their time.
- Use open-ended questions.
- Express empathy and acceptance.
- Roll with resistance.
- Avoid argumentation.

What Are Some Ways to Deal with an Angry Parent/Guardian?

Some parents/guardians may have very strong feelings about their child's use of alcohol or other drugs. In some cases, it may be necessary for you to allow the parents/guardians to tell their story or to vent some unpleasant feelings before the interview. Let them detail these complaints and frustrations and ask for clarification. Provide suggestions only when asked to do so. Do not argue with the parents/guardians, and avoid personalizing the anger-provoking behavior. Maintain your focus on the interview. Try to understand their point of view and keep focused on the task at hand. Be objective and accept any insight they might have as to why their child is using. Try to hear them and understand their feelings and position wih regard to this issue. If necessary, reschedule the interview for a later date. If they become abusive or direct their anger toward you, end the interview.

Here are three main messages that parents can communicate to their son or daughter about drug use:

1. Many young people are choosing abstinence, which is a safe and acceptable choice.

2. We don't want you to use alcohol before you are legal to do so, and we don't want you to use tobacco or other drugs in any way.

3. If you choose to use alcohol when you are of legal drinking age, we want you to do so cautiously and properly.

Recommended Guidelines

- Using alcohol or other drugs is a personal choice—don't let anyone pressure you to use them.

- Alcohol and other drugs are not necessary to have a good time.

- Using illegal drugs can cause legal and serious health risks, including death.

- Prescription medications should be used only as directed and *never* with other drugs or alcohol.

What Are Risk and Protective Factors?

Parents and guardians can do many things to help keep a young person from using alcohol and other drugs. (A parent guide that expands on this topic is on the CD-ROM.) Things that *can cause* an adolescent to use are called *risk factors* (because they are putting the youth at risk). Things that *can prevent* an adolescent from using are called *protective factors* (because these help to protect the youth from risk). The following lists include examples of each of these.

Risk Factors of Personality

- internalizing: a belief that success is due to hard work and ability

- externalizing: a belief that success is due to luck or easy work

- irritability: bad temper, bad mood

- impulsiveness: act without thinking first

- reduced attention span: easily distracted, difficult to focus on work

- aggressiveness: violent, destructive, act in the "heat of passion"

- "emotional" tendencies: moody, up and down, excitable, high-strung

- childhood diagnosis of a mental health disorder (for example, ADHD)

Risk Factors of Environment

- stressful events: a death in the family, an accident, or health problems
- lack of support and supervision: kids who are left alone without an adult around
- deviant peer groups: friends who get into trouble at school or in the community
- social and cultural norms: rules of religion, society, or culture
- socioeconomic factors: not enough money or too much
- neighborhood: many neighbors who use alcohol and/or other drugs

Protective Factors

Protective factors are people, activities, and skills that help prevent an adolescent from using alcohol or other drugs. The more protective factors the better. Some protective factors are

- a supportive family
- non-using peers
- positive role models (for example, coaches, teachers, clergy, extended family)
- a connection with one's school (for example, band, team sports, clubs)
- having hobbies or other positive activities outside of school
- a positive self-image and self-esteem
- social skills training
- academic competence and success
- being resilient in cases of high risk, stress, or traumatic events
- participating in a Head Start program at an early age

What Cognitive Variables Are Related to Changing Behavior?

Sometimes adolescents have learned distorted beliefs regarding their substance-use behavior. These distortions become negative patterns of thinking that can continue throughout one's lifetime. In order to help the youth change, it is important to discover these misperceptions in their thinking and cognitive processes. The following four cognitive variables are relative to changes in one's behavior (Monti, Colby, and O'Leary 2001).

- *Reasons for using:* Some young people believe that by using alcohol or other drugs they will become more popular and accepted among their peers.

- *What they expect from using:* To escape; to reduce stress, anxiety, and/or depression; to be more socially accepted; and to "get high" are all expectations that may be held by adolescents with regard to their use of alcohol or other drugs.

- *How ready they are to change their behavior:* This ranges from not wanting to change, to thinking about change, to trying to change, to making an effort to change, and finally changing while attempting to remain sober without relapse. This specific area is where the analysis of the costs and benefits of using is helpful.

- *Self-efficacy:* Personal confidence, self-esteem, and self-motivation are continually influential. The level of self-efficacy in an individual has been noted to affect one's choices and path in life, as well as one's capability to choose a positive path. Helping adolescents to recognize that they are worthy of a better life that includes sobriety is one small way of making the difference.

Each one of these areas plays an important role in the substance-related behavior of adolescents. It is meaningful to guide youths as they open up and discuss the specific areas that are causing them the most difficulty. In accomplishing this task, they are better able to recognize where they need to do the most work and where they have the most support.

Resources

This section contains an index of websites and other resources that may be of interest to service providers who are seeking additional information concerning the treatment of adolescent drug abuse.

National Websites

www.abovetheinfluence.com—Encourages decision making in young people

www.drugfree.org—Resources to help parents prevent, intervene, and find treatment for their children

www.theantidrug.com—Teaches how to talk to your kids about drugs

www.laantidroga.com—Teaches how to talk to your kids about drugs in Spanish

www.teachersguide.org—Drug prevention resources and classroom activities

www.mediacampaign.org—Resources and links for Media Campaign partners, community groups, and the media

www.whitehousedrugpolicy.gov—Policies and research information of the Office of National Drug Council Policy

www.findtreatment.samhsa.gov—Finding a treatment facility near you

www.ncadd.org—Substance abuse resources provided by the National Council on Alcohol and Drug Dependence

www.nida.nih.gov—National Institute on Drug Abuse

www.samhsa.gov—Substance Abuse and Mental Health Services Administration

www.monitoringthefuture.org—The University of Michigan site for "Monitoring the Future," an annual survey of student substance use

www.casacolumbia.org—Website of The National Center on Addiction and Substance Abuse (CASA) at Columbia University, providing various resources that include research on the effects substance abuse and addiction have on the nation's most serious problems, and surveys of the attitudes of teens, parents, teachers, and principals toward alcohol and other drug use

Free Publications and National Resources

1. *The Office of National Drug Control Policy:* This is the office that coordinates drug policy throughout the federal government. Their website is www.whitehousedrugpolicy.gov. Their toll-free number is (800) 666-3332. Calling this number will connect you with a representative of the National Clearinghouse for Alcohol and Drug Information, a federal government agency. You may order from a vast number of *free* publications for educators, parents, and young people.

2. *The National Council on Alcoholism and Drug Dependence, Inc. (NCADD):* This is a voluntary health organization offering services, publications, and information. To contact them, write to 244 East 58th Street, 4th Floor, New York, NY 10022, or call (800) NCA-CALL. Their website is www.ncadd.org.

3. *Drug Strategies:* This is a nonprofit institute that publishes "Treating Teens: A Guide to Adolescent Drug Programs," which compares and evaluates drug treatment programs. To contact them, write to 1616 P Street NW, Suite 220, Washington, DC 20036, or call (202) 939-0664. Their website is www.drugstrategies.com.

References

American Psychiatric Association. 2013. *Diagnostic and statistical manual of mental disorders (DSM-5).* 5th ed. Washington, D.C.: American Psychiatric Association.

Bien, T. H., W. R. Miller, and J. S. Tonigan. 1993. Brief interventions for alcohol problems: A review. *Addiction* 88: 315–36.

Breslin, C., L. Selina, K. Sdao-Jarvie, E. Tupker, and V. Ittig-Deland. 2002. Brief treatment for young substance abusers: A pilot study in an addiction treatment setting. *Psychology of Addictive Behaviors* 16: 10–16.

Centre for Addiction and Mental Health, Virtual Resource for the Addiction Treatment System. 1999a. A *curriculum guide.* Available online at www.camh.net/publications/index.html.

———. 1999b. *A parent and community handbook.* 4th ed. Available on-line at www.camh.net/publications/index.html.

Chung, T., and C. S. Martin. 2011. Prevalence and clinical course of adolescent substance use and substance use disorders. In *Clinical manual of adolescent substance abuse treatment.* Edited by Y. Kaminer and K. C. Winters. Washington, D.C.: American Psychiatric Association.

Clark, D., and O. Bukstein. 1998. Psychopathology in adolescent alcohol abuse and dependence. *Alcohol Health and Research World* 22: 117–21.

Clark, D., and K. C. Winters. 2002. Measuring risks and outcomes in substance use disorders prevention research. *Journal of Consulting and Clinical Psychology* 70: 1207–23.

Clayton, R. R. 1992. Transitions in drug use: Risk and protective factors. In *Vulnerability to drug abuse.* Edited by M. D. Glantz and R. W. Pickens. Washington, D.C.: American Psychological Assocation.

Erickson, S. J., M. Gerstle, and S. W. Feldstein. 2005. Brief interventions and motivational interviewing with children, adolescents, and their parents in pediatric health care settings. *Archives of Pediatric Adolescent Medicine* 159: 1173–80.

Fromme, K., and E. J. D'Amico. 2000. Measuring adolescent alcohol outcome expectancies. *Psychology of Addictive Behaviors* 14: 206–12.

Galanter, M., and H. Kleber, eds. 1999. *The American Psychiatric Press textbook of substance abuse treatment.* Washington, D.C.: American Psychiatric Press.

Hettema, J., J. Steele, and W. R. Miller. 2005. Motivational interviewing. *Annual Review of Clinical Psychology* 1: 91–111.

Institute of Medicine. 1990. *Broadening the base of treatment for alcohol problems.* Washington, D.C.: National Academy Press.

Lawson, G., J. Peterson, and A. Lawson. 1983. *Alcoholism in the family: A guide to treatment and prevention.* Gaithersburg, Md.: Aspen Publishers.

Lawson, G. W., and A. W. Lawson. 1992. *Adolescent substance abuse: Etiology, treatment, and prevention.* Gaithersburg, Md.: Aspen Publishers.

Miller, W. R., and S. Rollnick. 2002. *Motivational interviewing: Preparing people to change addictive behavior.* 2nd ed. New York: Guilford Press.

Miller, W. R., and V. C. Sanchez. 1993. Motivating young adults for treatment and lifestyle change. In *Issues in alcohol use and misuse by young adults.* Edited by G. Howard. Notre Dame, Ind.: University of Notre Dame Press.

Monti, P. M., S. M. Colby, and T. A. O'Leary. 2001. *Adolescents, alcohol, and substance abuse: Reaching teens through brief interventions.* New York: Guilford Press.

Peck, D. G. 1983. Legal and social factors in the deterrence of adolescent marijuana use. *Journal of Alcohol and Drug Education* 28, no. 3: 58–74.

Prochaska, J. O., C. C. DiClemente, and J. C. Norcross. 1992. In search of how people change: Applications to addictive behaviors. *American Psychologist* 47: 1102–14.

Sampl, S., and R. Kadden. 2001. *Motivational enhancement therapy and cognitive behavioral therapy for adolescent cannabis users: 5 sessions.* Cannabis Youth Treatment Series, vol. 1. U.S. Department of Health and Human Services, Substance Abuse and Mental Health Services Administration, Center for Substance Abuse Treatment. DHHS publication no. (SMA) 01-3486.

Segal, B., F. Cromer, H. Stevens, and P. Wasserman. 1982. Patterns of reasons for drug use among detained and adjudicated juveniles. *International Journal of the Addictions* 17, no. 7: 1117–30.

Shaffer, D. R. 1993. *Developmental psychology: Childhood and adolescence.* 3d ed. Belmont, Calif.: Brooks/Cole Publishing Company.

Svendsen, R. 2001. *Walking the talk: A program for parents about alcohol, tobacco and other drug use and nonuse.* 2d ed. Anoka, Minn.: Minnesota Institute of Public Health.

U.S. Department of Health and Human Services, National Institutes of Health, National Institute on Alcohol Abuse and Alcoholism. 1995. *Cognitive-behavioral coping skills therapy manual.* Project MATCH Series, vol. 3. NIH publication number 94-3724.

U.S. Department of Health and Human Services, National Institutes of Health, National Institute on Drug Abuse. 2001. *Hallucinogens and dissociative drugs: Including LSD, PCP, ketamine, dextromethorphan.* Research Report Series. NIH publication number 01-4209.

U.S. Department of Health and Human Services, Substance Abuse and Mental Health Services Administration, Center for Substance Abuse Treatment. 1999a. *Brief interventions and brief therapies for substance abuse treatment.* Treatment Improvement Protocols (TIPs), no. 34. Order no. BKD341.

———. 1999b. *Treatment for adolescents with substance use disorders.* Treatment Improvement Protocols (TIPs), no. 32. Order no. BKD307.

———. 2000. *Enhancing motivation for change in substance abuse treatment.* Treatment Improvement Protocols (TIPs), no. 35. Order no. BKD342.

U.S. Department of Health and Human Services, Substance Abuse and
Mental Health Services Administration, National Clearinghouse for
Alcohol and Drug Information. 1999. *Tips for teens: The truth about
methamphetamine.*

Vernon, A., and R. H. Al-Mabik. 1995. *What growing up is all about: A
parent's guide to child and adolescent development.* Champaign, Ill.:
Research Press.

Winters, K. C. 1999. Treating adolescents with substance use disorders: An
overview of practice issues and treatment outcomes. *Substance Abuse*
20: 203–25.

———. 2000. Monitoring access to treatment for adolescent drug abusers.
Poster presentation at the annual convention of the College on Problems
of Drug Dependence, San Juan, Puerto Rico.

About the Author

Ken Winters, Ph.D., is a professor in the Department of Psychiatry at the University of Minnesota, director of the Center for Adolescent Substance Abuse Research, and a senior scientist with the Treatment Research Institute, Philadelphia, Pennsylvania. He received his B.A. from the University of Minnesota and a Ph.D. in Psychology (Clinical) from the State University of New York at Stony Brook. His primary research interests are the assessment and treatment of addictions, including adolescent drug abuse and problem gambling. He is on the editorial board of the *Journal of Substance Abuse Treatment* and the *Journal of Child and Adolescent Substance Abuse,* and has received numerous research grants from the National Institutes of Health and various foundations. He was the 2008 recipient of the Research to Evidence-Based Practice Award from JMATE, a national organization on effective treatment for adolescents. Dr. Winters is a frequent speaker and trainer, and serves as a consultant to many organizations, including the Hazelden Foundation, The Partnership at Drugfree.org, the National Center for Responsible Gaming, and the Mentor Foundation (an international drug abuse prevention organization).